Alan Sked

The Case for Brexit

Dictus Publishing

Publisher:
Dictus Publishing
is a trademark of
Dodo Books Indian Ocean Ltd., member of the OmniScriptum S.R.L Publishing group
str. A.Russo 15, of. 61, Chisinau-2068, Republic of Moldova Europe
Printed at: see last page
ISBN: 978-620-2-47974-5

Bye Bye Brussels

Why Britain Should Quit the European Union

by Alan Sked,

Professor of International History and former Convenor of

European Studies at the London School of Economics.

Introduction

This book has been written by a liberal academic specialising in British and European diplomatic and intellectual history and is designed to provide an historical perspective on the debate over British membership of the EU. It analyses what is unique about European and British history before examining why Britain entered the EEC/EU in the first place. It then traces Britain's experience of EU membership before dissecting the present crisis in which the EU finds itself. Its concluding chapter provides an exposition of the case for Brexit.

The author is someone who has travelled widely in Europe and who studied in Vienna for his Oxford D.Phil. He has translated a book from Hungarian and commonly works with German, French and Italian documents in pursuing his research interests. His own books have been translated into several European languages. He is a passionate European but not a supporter of the EU, which he regards as an historical aberration.

1

The chapters of this book form an intellectual argument, which takes some knowledge of the EU for granted. However, for readers who are confused by the objectives and operating structures of the EU and the difficulties it now faces, an appendix has been added entitled *The European Union and its Decline: A Factual Explanation.* Some readers may wish to read this section first.

Chapter One: Europe

People often confuse the European Union with Europe. The first, of course, is a temporary political and economic arrangement between several European states, while the latter is a geographical area. The latter will always exist on maps. Whether that can be said of the EU remains to be seen. One is reminded of the Czech historian and statesman, Palacky's boast about his native Bohemia, namely that it had existed before the Habsburg Empire and would still exist after the latter had disappeared. I feel much the same about Great Britain and the EU.

Still, it cannot be denied that the EU, despite its present sad state, can have a weird effect on people. Take *Guardian* columnist Polly Toynbee, for example, whose articles regularly excoriate Tory ministers for grinding down the British working class for the benefit of big business. On 2 July 2014 her column included an appeal to the Labour Party before the 2015 general election to pander *'to every industrialist and financier as the only party to protect business interests'* in the EU. She also praised Ed Balls and Ed Miliband for their efforts to suck up to the City of London in the same context. Then there is that *cri de coeur* of September 2012 entitled *For Europe: Manifesto for a Postnational*

Revolution in Europe, written by Daniel Cohn-Bendit and Guy Verhofstadt. The first is the former student revolutionary leader of May 1968 in Paris who later confessed in a magazine interview that the 'events' of that year had signified 'nothing'; he now leads the Greens in the European Parliament no doubt with just as much significance. The second is a leader of Belgium's Liberals and another European Parliamentary notable. They too are struck by EU-mania and write in their manifesto: 'Only the European Union' can 'guarantee the social rights of all European citizens and eradicate poverty'. This will be welcome news to the 11% unemployed in the EU and the 40-50% of unemployed youth in Southern Europe. Again, they write, 'only Europe'—they confuse it with the EU—can solve the problems of globalization, climate change and social injustice. Their enthusiasm knows no bounds: 'no continent is better equipped to renounce its violent past and strive for a more peaceful world'. They state that should the euro fail, the whole EU project will fail too, with the result that 'two thousand years of history risk being wiped out.' In order to avoid such a catastrophe, a 'strong' authority is required in the EU to 'enforce compliance'. Presumably they can now thank God for Angela Merkel, Germany's *Schmerzdame* or dominatrix in the apt phrase of Germany's *Stern* magazine. Curiously enough, even the Greeks themselves remain in thrall to the EU and the euro, despite all their hardships and national humiliation during the recent bailout negotiations. They certainly repudiated their own anti-austerity referendum result by backing the U-turn by their premier Alexis Tsipras, when, faced with the prospect of Greece being expelled from the EU and the Eurozone, he opted for 'compliance' supervised by Berlin after all. Seventy per cent of Greeks, according to opinion polls, want to remain in the Eurozone at any price. And it will be a huge one.

Another example of EU-mania could be found in Scotland in 2014 during the referendum campaign for 'Scottish independence'. The ruling party in Scotland, the SNP or Scottish National Party, campaigned not just for an independent Scotland but 'an independent Scotland in a federal Europe'. As readers will understand, this is a contradiction in terms, an oxymoron. Still, amazing as it seems, Alex Salmond, the SNP leader, advocated Scottish 'independence' on the basis of a currency (which had still to be decided) but would definitely not be Scottish (he hoped the Bank of England would go back on its adamant refusal and allow an Anglo-Scottish currency union based on the pound sterling to go ahead); he obscured the fact that there would be no Scottish passport (but an EU one); he failed to mention that Scots law would be subordinated to EU law (hence no Scottish sovereignty); failed, too, to mention that most laws for Scotland would henceforth originate in Brussels; and did not explain how a mere six Scottish MEPs in a European Parliament of 751 members, with no Scottish Commissioner, and next to no votes in European Council decisions, could possibly defend Scottish national interests. Insofar as the pro-EU unionist parties in the UK had anything to say about the EU dimension of the debate, it was to point out that a newly independent Scotland would have to apply to be admitted to the EU in the first place—an application which might well prove unacceptable to member states with their own breakaway regions. Salmond of course brushed aside all such objections as fantasy. He also attempted to brush aside predictions of a dire economic future under independence by forecasting a golden age of prosperity buoyed by decades of North Sea oil revenue at a price of $130 a barrel. Only one year later the price was a mere $45 a barrel and oil revenues over the next twenty years are now predicted to amount to only a couple of billion pounds in total. Had the referendum succeeded, Scotland, lacking both subsidies from the UK

Exchequer and North Sea oil revenues, would now be in absolutely dire straits. Even in 2014 its national deficit would have been 8% of GDP, since in that year Scotland spent £66 billion and raised only £54 billion in revenue. If it had been accepted as a member of the EU it would now be forced to swallow the same medicine as Greece and would be run by the *troika* rather than the SNP (Sham (?) National Party). It, too, would be subject to a *Diktat* by the *Schmerzdame*, although when all this was pointed out to Salmond in the House of Commons, where, ironically, he is now a British MP, he merely responded: 'we are pro-European!' Perhaps, he should just have declared: 'we want to be a German colony!' Despite the expected run-down of North Sea oil and the dismantling of oil rigs, his party, amazingly, is still threatening to re-run the referendum. Scottish education is clearly not what it used to be— just witness, for example, the recent controversies over Scottish universities, Scottish schools and the place of the latter in international league tables--and I say this as a proud Scot with a university degree from an ancient Scottish university. (For a brief overview of the economic prospects of an 'independent' Scotland', see the article by David Smith in the *Sunday Times* of 13 September 2015 entitled 'The Great Escape: how Scotland dodged a bullet'.) The situation in Scotland is all the more curious given the research findings of the National Centre of Social Research based on its British Social Attitudes and Scottish Social Attitudes surveys. These cast grave doubts on the SNP assumption that Scots feel more pro-European than the English. The 'NatCen' report reveals that in 2014 only 9% of Scots described themselves as European compared with 15% of people in the UK as a whole. The *Times* on 28 October 2015 reported these findings under the headline 'Scots "don't feel as European" as the rest of the UK'.

If Alex Salmond and his followers turn out to be bastard Bravehearts, there are others in Europe who *have* shown the courage to be masters of their own destiny: the Icelanders. As Matt Ridley put it in one of his characteristically brilliant columns in the *Times* on 29 July 201: 'Iceland teaches a very acute lesson for Greece, Britain, Europe and the world: independence works.'

In 2008 Iceland like Greece suffered a dreadful financial crash yet the country is now growing rapidly, running trade and budget surpluses, with minimal unemployment and strong pension funds. A settlement with the creditors of its failed three banks is imminent and credit controls will soon be lifted. As Ridley tells it, the country's fundamental advantages (fish, tourism, geothermal energy and an educated workforce) were untouched by the crisis. Thus, with the help of a devaluation of 60%, Iceland started working through austerity to prosperity. It cut public spending, hiked interest rates and, at the behest of the IMF, introduced exchange controls to contain inflation. Tourist numbers have doubled in five years and fish catches are at a record high.

Ridley also points out that whereas Scottish and Swiss banks were larger than Iceland's compared to GDP (and Iceland's banking sector was nine times its economic output), the world chose to save Scottish and Swiss banks while letting those of Iceland collapse. Iceland was simply left to its fate. The US Federal Reserve refused the country a currency swap (while offering it to other Nordic states); Britain's Gordon Brown declared Iceland bankrupt and froze the assets of its banks in the UK using anti-terrorism legislation; he also compensated British investors in Icesave, the overseas branch of one of its biggest banks and sent the bill to the Icelandic government. The Icelanders, however, refused to pay (after holding two referendums) and their case was later upheld by the court of the European Free Trade Area. This small country, with a population only half the size of Cardiff, was not to be intimidated. Positioned outside all the great trading blocks and nations and spurned by all of them, it proved that there is no safe have in a larger entity and that it is best to be master of one's own fate.

Iceland, according to Ridley, had two great advantages. It could devalue its own currency and was outside the dreadful European Common Fisheries Policy. In short its fishermen could manage its own fish quotas and fish stocks properly. It was also outside the EU and was therefore exempt from the EU's common external tariff. This means it can trade freely with the rest of the world as well as the EU and last year it signed its own free-trade treaty with China. True it has to abide by EU rules if it exports to the EU but it has to apply US rules when it exports there. If it does not export, it applies no rules. Ridley adds: 'Iceland represents itself on the World Trade Organization, whereas Britain is represented mainly by the EU trade commissioner, a Swede. The notion that being outside the EU means you don't get to write the rules of world trade is back to front. The EU is increasingly at the mercy of others' rules set at the supranational level anyway: regaining our independence would increase our influence there.'

According to Ridley, Iceland's entire history confirms the benefits of independence and he concludes his article: "Iceland reminds us that size does not matter nearly as much as most politicians pretend. Small countries often thrive. Look at New Zealand, Singapore, Estonia, Kuwait. They can be that much more nimble in their decisions. And if a country of 320,000 people can have the confidence to thrive alone in the North Atlantic, trading with the EU but not enmeshed in it, why on earth cannot the world's fifth largest economy?' Indeed, why not?

Clearly Greeks had various reasons to want to remain in the EU. For most people these would have been practical: the fear that a return to the drachma would impose intolerable economic burdens on top of those that had already been suffered to remain inside the Eurozone; the need to remain inside an association of democratic nations after the experience of military rule under the colonels between 1967 and 1974; the fear of relapsing into political extremism of left or right once again, given the legacy of the Greek Civil War after 1947. But also at play was the idea that the EU represented the West or European civilization, whereas Greece, left alone would regress to mere Balkan status or worse still, might become something like a failed Middle Eastern state---its legacy of century-long Ottoman occupation being relevant here. As will be seen, many states had very particular objectives in joining the EEC/EU, aims which still motivate their desire to remain within it, although there has also always been, hovering in the background, the propaganda that the EU does represent Western or European civilization. This is a myth that needs to be deconstructed.

My late colleague at LSE, Professor Alan Milward published a book in 1992 entitled *The European Rescue of the Nation State*. It helped to shift the emphasis in European studies away from ideological and theoretical analyses of European integration to more practical concerns. For example, he argued that states pursued their national interests in European negotiations rather than beliefs or principles. Thus France in promoting the Schuman Plan was more concerned to obtain cheap German coking coal from the Ruhr in order to implement the Monnet Plan for French reconstruction and to break up German coal and steel monopolies than in simply furthering principles of European federalism. Italy, similarly, was concerned to acquire iron ores from French colonies in North Africa. Far from destroying the nation-state, Milward saw European integration as helping to rescue it after the ravages of war and occupation and would later write that in Western Europe, the nation-state reached its apogee in the mid-1960s. After all, the basic functions of the nation state were the preservation of internal order and the defence of frontiers against external attack; the provision of 'legitimate' government through the preservation of an established state structure including national symbols and institutions, which gave citizens a sense of participation in the democratic life of the state; the provision of services including welfare services which made citizens feel part of a national community; and the use of primarily Keynesian economic policy to sustain economic growth. From this perspective, the nation-state did not come under real attack from federalism till the mid-1980s, since when (I would argue) the effects, political, economic and constitutional, have been clearly deleterious.

In a sense, what Milward was pointing out was self-evident. Many states had obvious national interests to pursue in joining the EEC/EU. West Germany desperately sought *Gleichberechtigung* or equality of treatment after the horrors of her Nazi past and defeat in war; France wished once again to protect herself from any revival of German nationalism; the Low Countries were economically dependent on France and Germany; and Italy wanted to revive her claim to be a major European power. Later on, Spain, Portugal and Greece, after having cast off their dictatorships, sought comfort in the company of Western democracies, while after the downfall of the Soviet Empire, the East European and Baltic States sought the protection of EU membership against any sort of revival of Soviet/Russian ambitions. So far, so self-evident. Bismarck, after all, had once remarked: 'I have always found the word "Europe" in the mouths of those politicians who wanted from other powers something they did not dare demand in their own name.' The odd-man out was Britain. Even General de Gaulle could never understand why Great Britain wanted to join the EEC. At his notorious press conference of January 1963 when he vetoed the first British application to join, he asked why Britain, which had democratic institutions, a Commonwealth, and cheap food imported from all over the world, would want to join the EEC? England, he said, 'is maritime, she is linked through her exchanges, her markets, her supply lines to the most diverse and often the most distant countries; she pursues essentially industrial and commercial activities and only slightly agricultural ones. She has in all her doings very marked and very original habits and traditions.' He was too polite and too French to add that she was still a world power and had been a victor in the Second World War. What he did add was that her entry would change the nature of the Community which would inevitably come under US dominance. He knew, therefore, why Britain's application should be vetoed but could not understand why it should have been be submitted in the first place. In fact, that is still a mystery to which we shall have to return later. In the meantime, it is necessary to deconstruct the major myth still vaguely associated with the EU, that somehow it represents the climax of European civilization.

This is indeed the—often unstated-- belief of all those who like to think of themselves as 'good Europeans', something that the rest of us are always urged to become. Their belief system includes the myth that the EU encapsulates the best of European history, so that those who reject the EU are somehow 'bad Europeans'. Today, the trope is less in evidence than it once was, thanks to the recent lacklustre record of the EU in financial and foreign policy matters, but it often resurfaces. At the heart of the matter is European exceptionalism, which is based on a reading of European history which is blatantly selective. British history used to suffer from the same sort of thing— the Whig interpretation of British history in which British parliamentary democracy broadened over the centuries through judicious reforms to include votes for everyone and welfare for all. This admirable domestic history was rewarded in foreign affairs with victory in war over all sorts of nasty—and mainly European—enemies. America has its equivalent in the concept of American exceptionalism, to which every successful US presidential candidate adheres, and indeed must adhere. It is the story of America as the shining city on a hill, the land of God's chosen people who, having established democracy at home have always been generous enough to spread and defend it across a globe, whose freedom still depends in the last resort on American armed forces. Part of the belief system of American exceptionalism is the conviction that in the USA and probably only in the USA can anyone rise to the top by sheer hard work and individual enterprise. Thus America is 'the land of the free and the home of the brave'. Indeed, during the early Cold War, many Americans were hounded by a congressional body called the House Un-American Activities Committee which condemned as 'un-American' all those who basically did not believe in American exceptionalism. This sounds strange to us. After all what would it mean to be 'un-British'? (Gordon Brown's attempts to define Britishness led nowhere.) Yet Americans today will know immediately what is meant by the adjective 'un-American'.

In the 1960s, it was also quite common to believe in 'good' and 'bad' Germans. Unfortunately, probably the only 'good German' known abroad was Herr Willy Brandt. Again the phrase was historically determined. 'Good Germans' were those who had resisted Hitler and the Nazis—which left an awful lot of people who did not. The term 'bad Germans', out of politeness, was almost never used, save *in extremis*. But the division existed. In the world of communism, finally, there were 'good' and 'bad' communists. 'Bad' communists were those who betrayed Soviet Russia either by design or by failing to recognise the latest configuration of the 'co-relation of forces'. They were usually purged or expelled.

Let us return, however, to European exceptionalism and 'good Europeans'. These are really just European nationalists but like all nationalists require a mythological view of their past in order to sustain their political beliefs. The only difference between them and other nationalists is that they repudiate nationalism. They do so under the delusion that nationalism always causes wars and that as a concept, it presupposes linguistic and cultural unity. However, there are large and small multilingual nations—Switzerland, Canada, Spain, Belgium and India for example—and cultural unity can be manufactured--just as it was in the case of several European states. The key is history and it is no coincidence that the EU Commission has been at work for decades promoting a version of European history that appeals to 'good Europeans', who, consciously or unconsciously, subscribe to a number of myths.

First, as already mentioned, there is the myth that the EU transcends nationalism; secondly that Europe is not, as Bismarck maintained, a 'geographical expression' but a cultural unity formed from shared historical experience. This experience is a cumulative one which begins with the ancient Greeks and thereafter follows a peculiarly 'civilized' route through history via ancient Rome, 'Christianity', the Renaissance, the Enlightenment, and the French Revolution and despite the setbacks of two world wars, comes to a climax with the creation of the European Union. This is the 'two thousand years of history' threatened with wipe-out, referred to by Cohn-Bendit and Verhofstadt in their 2012 *Manifesto.* Once the EU is transformed into a federal state, it will further this historical evolution by enthroning Reason in the world, thus saving it from American materialism, Chinese communism and Islamic fundamentalism. Certainly, this is what Habermas seems to believe. A third myth is that Europe has been the creation of a number of great idealists , headed by Jean Monnet, but that the idealism of these continental statesman has always been frustrated by Great Britain led by 'bad Europeans' who are determined to stop the creation of a federal Europe. Yet a federal, united Europe should take its rightful place in the world and hold the world's balance of power. After all the USA is the offspring of Europe as is Latin America. Communism in all its forms is the bastard child of European socialism, while Third World nationalism is again the product of European thought. For much of the previous millennium Europe dominated the world in terms of ideology, technology and politics. It is only natural, therefore, that Europe should resume its rightful position at the centre of world affairs and not leave it to the mercy of the superpowers.

Let us now examine these myths. The idea that nationalism always causes war is clearly unsustainable. Nationalism, after all, has many advantages: it reconciles classes; smooths over regional differences; and gives people a sense of community, identity and history. European federalists/nationalists are themselves seeking precisely these benefits from the EU, which, far from transcending nationalism, behaves just like a large, albeit artificial, nation-state. Moreover, a strict reading of European history would suggest that it was the refusal of supranational dynastic states---the Ottoman, Habsburg and Napoleonic empires—to allow for national self-determination that brought about wars. Likewise, in the twentieth century, it was the Kaiser's bid for world power (*Griff nach der Weltmacht* in Fritz Fischer's famous phrase) and Hitler's racial mumbo-jumbo which led to world conflict. In short it has been opposition to nation-states and the yearning for continental-power bases which led to conflict in the past and more than once to the near-destruction of European civilization. Moreover, even when states come together, there is no guarantee that they will stay together. The greatest war in US history was its

Civil War. Almost all the colonial federations given independence by the British crown later fell apart. Holland and Belgium separated after their union. So, too, did Norway and Sweden. Czechoslovakia is now two states: the Czech Republic and Slovakia. Yugoslavia imploded violently at the end of the twentieth century, while even the USSR, a modern super-state, is no more. Peoples feel much more comfortable in nation-states, which, by their very nature, encourage community, democracy, identity and patriotism. Free trade and mutual defence arrangements between normal nation-states, therefore, offer a more permanent path to peace and prosperity than an artificial union or modern version of empire.

'European civilization', the next myth, seems more real for many people. But ask them to define it and they are often at a loss. When Mahatma Ghandi was asked his view of the matter, he responded, famously by saying that it might be a good idea. In fact, he had a very poor opinion of Europe, stating: 'It is my firm opinion that Europe does not represent the spirit of God and Christianity but the spirit of Satan. And Satan's successes are the greatest when he appears with the name of God on his lips.' Beware of Europeans bearing gifts was his sage advice and we should certainly take it with regard to the federalists.

As Ghandi would have been the first to admit, however, Europeans are different from Africans, Indians, Chinese and Arabs. Basically, of course, this is merely an ethnic or geographical notion, the same in fact which used to excite 'white men' in remote lands among primitive tribes. In this sense, of course, 'European' includes American, since Americans in the nineteenth century were regarded as just another branch of the white race.

On the other hand, since America's rise to world power, Europeans have become keener to firm up their ideas about exactly what it is that makes them European—hence the much-invoked historical odyssey from Ancient Greece

(Athens, of course, not Sparta) to modern Brussels. The objections to this way of interpreting Europe's past are fairly obvious. It is so obviously selective— and on a variety of levels—that it clearly draws on propaganda rather than history. There really is little point in treating European history as if the Greeks only existed in ancient times (how Brussels today must wish that that were true!), as if fascism and national socialism were not integral parts of the story, or as if Christianity did not divide Europeans as much as it united them.

It is not even plausible to claim Greece, Rome and Christianity as essentially European civilizations. Greece and Rome were Mediterranean cultures with major centres in Africa, Asia Minor and the Near East. Alexander the Great, it should be remembered set out to conquer the civilized world in Egypt, Persia and India. He was unaware that he was doing so in the cause of European civilization. Greece and Rome were followed by other Mediterranean civilizations—Byzantium and the Turks. Byzantium was, like the Western Roman Empire after Constantine, a Christian power. Yet Christianity, it should be recalled, arose in Palestine from Jewish roots and was thus a Mediterranean religion. Although Christianity spread, it did so in a manner that divided Europeans as much as it united them. The Eastern Church refused to recognise the leadership of Rome, which leadership after the Reformation was also rejected by much of Western Europe. The result was that Russia and parts of Eastern and Southern Europe developed a different culture from that of Western and Central Europe, while for centuries religious wars and rivalries would divide the Continent. Meanwhile, the Mediterranean tradition still survived. The Turks were only slowly driven out of Europe (the battle of Lepanto in 1517; the siege of Vienna in 1683; the Balkan Wars of 1912-13) although even today they are members of NATO and candidates for full membership of the EU. When the great French historian, Ferdinand Braudel, came to write on the age of Philip II, he chose the title for his book, *La Mediterranée et le monde mediterranéan à l'epoque de Philippe II*. He did not write about the European civilization of that era. Finally, despite the pretensions of French statesmen and scholars, it is difficult to see the French Revolution as a unifying force in European history. Instead, it unleashed wars and ideological struggles all over the continent.

Europe, in truth, has been the home of many civilizations, often at the same time and with mixed results for the human race. It is facile and unhistorical to pretend that they have been a cumulative or unifying force. To quote a historian who gave much thought to this matter (Geoffrey Barraclough in his *History in a Changing World*, Oxford, 1955, p. 231): 'The extraordinarily impressive portrait head of Yarim-Lun, King of Alalakh in the eighteenth century BC, the Hermes of Praxiteles and Raphael's Sistine Madonna, are not stages in a continuous development towards artistic perfection; each is the expression of a distinct civilization.' The same is true of Egyptian pyramids, Doric temples and Gothic cathedrals as far as architecture is concerned. And the same is true once again regarding literature. Aristophanes, Virgil, Shakespeare, Goethe and Dostoevsky are not links in a chain. They do not add up to 'European culture' but reflect different European cultures. Today it is difficult even to talk of a contemporary European culture. Europeans read their national newspapers and watch national television programmes. Over and above that they may dine in Chinese or Indian restaurants (not to mention MacDonald's) or watch American films, soap operas and pop videos. They belong therefore both to their national cultures and to a cosmopolitan Western one based on jeans and junk food. To state that they belong to a specifically European culture is to indulge an act of faith. Nor should we lose sight of the fact that the growth of Muslim populations in many of Europe's cities—especially the biggest ones—will have an inescapable impact on European culture in the future.

The last of the myths of the European nationalists enumerated above included their belief that the world needs a European federal super-state to maintain a rational balance of power in the world. The relationship between Europe and the superpowers feels unnatural to many European federalists. After all since the time of the Renaissance, Europe has been at the centre of world affairs— voyages of discovery, colonial acquisitions, rising living standards, agrarian and agricultural revolutions, modern theories of government, world empires, the spreading of 'civilization' and much else. Russia during this time had to 'catch up' with Western Europe, not dominate or threaten it. Until recently (1917 or 1945) even the USA had only a passive role to play in world affairs, being invited to redress the balance of the Old World only when the European balance had itself spun out of control. Before then the world had been expected to revolve around a European axis.

Until the recent world economic crisis of 2008-9, 'good Europeans' had begun to hope that that situation might soon begin to prevail again. US defeat in Vietnam, the Carter years, Iran-Contra, and the George W. Bush presidency led Europeans to decry the poor quality of American leadership (they gave credit for ending the Cold War to Gorbachev), while conveniently forgetting that even Western European countries had a very patchy record of governance during the same period, including dictatorships (Spain, Portugal and Greece), terrorism (Germany, Italy, Spain, Northern Ireland) and corruption scandals (France, Italy, Germany and others). If European 'experience' was called for, it was forgotten that 'European experience' had brought about super-power hegemony in the first place. Finally, Europeans in any case found it difficult to agree on anything. Even during the Cold war only some states of Europe were members of NATO, not all of them full members, while several preferred to remain neutral. France always took a separate stand with regard to the politics of oil and there were wide differences of opinion between the leading European states over almost all areas of the world. Still, for 'good Europeans', the situation would have been much better had only the wisdom of the EU's founding fathers—Monnet, de Gasperi, Adenauer, Schuman—idealists all—been followed instead of being continually frustrated by the British starting with Churchill and Eden. These people (read Hugo Young's *This Blessed Plot*) think of European history in much the same way as that of European Civilization or the Ascent of Man. Instead of the Stone Age leading to the Bronze Age, leading to the Iron Age leading to the Machine Age or Greece leading to Rome leading to Christianity, leading to the Renaissance, leading to the Enlightenment and to Modernity, we have the story of the Council of Europe leading to the Schuman Plan, leading to the Pleven Plan, leading to the Treaty of Rome, leading to the Single European Act, leading to the Maastricht treaty, leading to the Lisbon Treaty. The obvious destination of future European history is a United Europe. Yet although this plan has been carved out on tablets of stone in heaven, Britain, especially since the days of Mrs. Thatcher, has been offering satanic opposition to the forces of light.

Neither do such people ever consider whether the existence of a European super-power would improve the world. They take that for granted. Nor do they consider the costs involved. To be organised properly it would require infinitely more resources (revenues, bureaucrats, and armed forces, not to mention treaties, regulations and directives), centralization and uniformity. It would also have to assume more responsibilities around the world with no greater guarantee of being able to execute them successfully than previous superpowers. America, after all, has a rather mixed record in international affairs since 1945. She was unable to prevent the Soviet take-over of Eastern Europe; unable to create a United States of Europe; unable to escape a military commitment to Western Europe; unable to prevent a Communist take-over of China; unable to liberate the people of North Korea; unable to win the war in Vietnam; unable to save the Shah of Iran; or to rescue hostages in the Middle East. Her recent wars in Iraq and Afghanistan have hardly resulted in the establishment of stable, democratic governments there; and the outcome of her recent nuclear deal with Iran cannot yet be determined. The Soviet Union, for her part, had a miserable record in international affairs. No advanced country in the world freely accepted her leadership and apart from occupied Eastern Europe she ended up with influence only in Cuba, South Yemen, Ethiopia and North Korea. Putin's Russia today, just like Communist China, has no followers or true friends.

Among the potential super-states of the world, on the other hand, Europe is in a political and economic position similar to that of Japan. Her military profile is limited and her world role is less than it might well deserve to be. Why then give up this relatively favourable position for the role of stumbling giant? Just because Henry Kissinger did not know who to phone when he wanted to contact 'Europe'? Why not allow the Kissingers of the world to remain baffled?

Europe already has defence arrangements under NATO, which, given the additional resources required to bring them up to date, should be sufficient to meet her needs. If she wants greater growth economically and more political satisfaction she would be well advised to ditch all plans for a federal Europe and create a Europe-wide free trade area which would allow independent sovereign states to cooperate economically and politically while remaining strong national democracies with governments clearly and directly responsible to their national electorates. These states could then quite easily make intergovernmental arrangements for student exchanges, reciprocal health service arrangements and provision for free movement of people insofar as each state found this desirable. There would be no need for 'none-fits-all' federalist regulations and directives.

Such an alternative Europe, moreover, would be absolutely in line with a true history of Europe. So let me explain.

There is indeed something special and wonderful about Europe, something that excited Europeans from the eighteenth century. Mazzini, the Italian patriot (although also a revolutionary and terrorist) when he founded a league of national revolutionary movements called *Young Europe*, in 1834 declared: 'Europe is the lever of the world. Europe is the land of liberty. Europe controls the universe. Here is the mission of progressive development that encompasses humanity.' He may sound like Cohn-Bendit and Verhofstadt but he was writing almost two centuries before them. What they have in common, however, is the belief that Europe is the home of progress. When my old Oxford doctoral supervisor A.J.P.Taylor wrote a brilliant review essay for *The New York Review of Books* on the theme of European unity back in March 1965 entitled *Snakes in Iceland*, he pointed out: '[Europeans] have also developed special ideas. They believe, for instance in progress. They expect everything to get better all the time. For them History is a record of improvement, not merely a record of events. They attach some importance to the Individual, an idea that has broadened into various forms of Democracy, Freedom and even Socialism. The rest of the world has followed their example in ideas also. Wherever you may be, you only have to look out of your hotel window, and you will see people dressed like Europeans, behaving like Europeans, thinking like Europeans.' One idea they never put up with, however, was European unity. To quote Taylor again: 'But if ever history has a lesson, European disunity is surely it. This is sad for men who advocate European unity and who yet, for professional or other reasons, wish to derive consoling lessons from history. A History of European Unity, if written without preconceptions, would resemble Dr. Johnson's favorite chapter. This was entitled "Chapter XXI. Snakes in Iceland," and read: "There are no snakes in Iceland."'

Taylor, as so often in his writings, had summed up whole schools of thought in a few witty lines. However, his paradox of boundless European self-confidence co-existing alongside a rejection of European unity will have to be explained.

If the late eighteenth century had given rise to the idea of progress, innumerable discoveries and scientific advances had consolidated it in the following century. And it was no illusion, as modern economic historians confirm. Stephen A. Schuker, for example, in his chapter in *Is There Still a West?* (University of Missouri Press, 2007), tells this now familiar tale as follows: 'In the year 1000 Western Europe could boast living standards no higher than those of the outside world. Indeed, since the fall of Rome, China, Japan and the Arab civilizations of the southern Mediterranean littoral had surpassed the West in technology and some aspects of material culture...combined gross domestic product grew three hundred –fold and per capita income thirteen fold over the next millennium, but the locus of growth reversed. By 1820 the West (conventionally defined as the thirteen Western and Northern European countries and the four leading British offshoots) had attained per capita income twice that of the rest of the world. From the late eighteenth century to the last quarter of the twentieth, the curve measuring progress turned upwards again. The West further differentiated itself from the rest of mankind in technological sophistication, health and the life expectancy, social welfare, and other indices of economic performance. By 2000 the per capita income gap between the West and the rest had increased to seven times.' Schuker concluded from these statistics: 'This advance in human well-being arguably ranks as the greatest achievement in the history of mankind. The United States and the richest European countries (as well as Japan and Singapore) currently enjoy average incomes twenty to thirty times greater than those of sub-Saharan Africa.' Schuker, an American, realises that most of the initial advances were European—roughly 80 percent of the world's chief intellectual and artistic accomplishments between 1400 and 1950 came from four countries or areas alone—England, France, Germany and Italy. Western Europe and the English-speaking off-shoots were unique in developing free-markets, security of property, a predictable system of law, and parliamentary limitations on the exercise of power. Western Europe in the sixteenth century also experienced a scientific revolution that not merely discredited traditional authority, but also gave leaders in every field—from soil chemistry to political theory—'the sense that they could master nature and improve on the wisdom of the ancients,' to quote Schuker once again.

The setback to European self-confidence as the centre of world progress occasioned by the two world wars but particularly by the first gave rise to movements aimed at making people aware once again of the idea of progress as European or Western civilization. Some of these actually called for European or world government. But it was among historians that the idea of European civilization as a progressive force was promoted most. In the United States, of course, the emphasis was on 'Western' rather than merely 'European' civilization. There the Contemporary Civilization course at Columbia College taught by people like John Herman Randall (author of the 1924 *The Making of the Modern Mind*) and the 'Great books' course at the University of Chicago, largely the brainchild of Robert Maynard Hutchins, concentrated on ideas and literature and the making of the Western mind. Also important was the multi-volume series written by Will Durant and his wife entitled *The Story of Civilization* which ran from 1935 to 1975 and eventually encompassed twelve volumes, nine thousand pages and four-and-a –half million words. This covered much more than ideas and literature but wove politics, sex, architecture, music, class, customs and just about everything into a stunning 'grand narrative' of the rise of Western civilization. The continuing need for such a narrative with its moral that the West meant freedom is the theme of David Gress's interesting work of 1998, *FROM PLATO TO NATO. The IDEA of the WEST and Its OPPONENTS*.

In Europe the *Cambridge Modern History* which was published between 1902 and 1912 fulfilled a rather similar task. True, it eschewed the ancient parts of the 'Grand Narrative' and started only with the age of discoveries but its fourteen volumes concentrated very much on the domestic and foreign policy history of the European states (including Britain) and their impact on the rest of the world. In this sense it gave its readers a sense of world history as being determined by the politics of Europe's great powers, representing the rise of civilization. After the First World War one of the greatest efforts to recreate this sense of a European or Western Civilization, now including the whole of the 'Grand Narrative' from Ancient Greece onwards, was that of F. S. Marvin, a Londoner, who after a distinguished career as an undergraduate at Oxford became first a schoolteacher, then an inspector of schools and finally Professor of Modern History at the Egyptian University. In 1913 his first book was published entitled *The Living Past: A Sketch of Western Progress*, which in 250 pages covered the history of Western Europe from prehistoric times till the present day. During the First World War he then began to organise lecture courses for teachers and others and between the wars he organised conferences around Europe –Vienna, Danzig, Stockholm and Prague—to promote his 'Unity History Schools, where lectures by leading scholars would be given on the theme of Western civilization and then published as volumes in his 'Unity Series' of books. Titles included *The Unity of Western Civilization, Progress and History, Recent Developments in European Thought, The Evolution of World Peace, Western Races and the World, Science and civilization, England and the World, Art and Civilization and The New World Order. The Unity of Western Civilization* included lectures by Earnest Barker, L.T. Hobhouse, J.W. Headley and J. A. Hobson and went through four editions. *The Evolution of World Peace* included lectures by Sir Paul Vinogradoff, H. W. C. Davis, G.N. Clark, G.P. Gooch, C.R. Beazley and H. G. Wells. The latter's lecture entitled 'An Apology for a World Utopia' began with the question: 'WHAT is the Utopian method?' and he answered it as follows: 'It is nothing more nor less than the method of planning.' He then asked: 'What is a Utopia?' and answered: 'It is a first sketch plan of a proposed replacement or change in human institutions,' adding: 'If a man is going to build a house the first thing he does is to make a sketch plan of the house he is going to build; if a factory has to be schemed or a ship designed, the most practical sorts of men do exactly what the Utopian does, they begin by making a vision of the thing they require.' Perhaps the EU Commission keeps a copy of this lecture at its headquarters in Brussels. The main thrust of all these writers was that the rise of Western or European civilization was the discovery of freedom among the ancient Greeks and its defence and consolidation as the centuries wore on. Freedom under the law, freedom to make contracts, freedom to trade, freedom from arbitrary arrest, freedom of the press, of assembly, freedom to vote taxes etc. etc. The emphasis was on philosophy and politics and law, although the Chicago school emphasised literature. The scientific revolution that Schuker noted was also acknowledged but the sheer scope of the economic transformation of the West in terms of economic growth after 1000 AD was overlooked, simply because economic historians had not yet discovered the cliometric tools and the sources needed to measure the changes involved.

The main arguments produced by these historians of Western civilization have often been extremely learned and subtle, and augmented by many other historians, have stood the test of time, at least insofar as they concentrated on the social, cultural, economic and technological changes witnessed over the centuries. Moreover, major challenges to this 'Grand Narrative' --Martin Bernal's *Black Athena. The Afroasiatic Roots of Classical Civilization* for example—have been shown to lack credibility. Still, there is another side to the coin. This includes not merely the criticisms of the myths of European civilization that have already been made but also other factors

European progress for many centuries encompassed slavery while it also took centuries to free Europe from the dead hand of feudal institutions, although both feudalism and slavery, it is true, were eventually left behind. Then there was the military superiority that European values bestowed on European armies. Ghandi would be very impressed by the quite remarkable book published in 2001 by the leading classicist and military historian, Victor David Hanson, namely *Why the West has Won. Carnage and Culture from Salamis to Vietnam.* Hanson begins his story with the tale of Xenophon's *Anabasis*--the history of 10,700 Greek mercenaries cut off in Persia in 401 BC who then fought their way back to Greece:

'The *Anabasis* makes it clear, however, that the Greeks fought much differently than their adversaries and that such unique Hellenic characteristics of battle— a sense of personal freedom, superior discipline, matchless weapons, egalitarian comeraderie, individual initiative, constant tactical adaptation and flexibility, preference for shock battle of heavy infantry—were themselves the murderous dividends of Hellenic culture at large. The peculiar way Greeks killed grew out of consensual government, equality among the middling classes, civilian audit of military affairs, and politics apart from religion, freedom and individualism, and rationalism. The ordeal of the Ten Thousand, when stranded and near extinction, brought out the polis that was innate in all Greek soldiers, who then conducted themselves on campaign precisely as civilians in their respective city-states.

In some form or another, the Ten Thousand would be followed by equally brutal European intruders: Agesilaus and his Spartans, Charles the mercenary captain, Alexander the Great, Julius Caesar and centuries of legionary dominance, the crusaders, Hernan Cortes, Portuguese explorers in Asiatic seas, British redcoats in India and Africa, and scores of other thieves, buccaneers, colonists, mercenaries, imperialists, and explorers. Most subsequent Western expeditionary forces were outnumbered and often deployed far from home. Nevertheless, they outfought their numerically superior enemies and in varying degrees drew on elements of Western culture to slaughter mercilessly their opponents.

In the long history of European military practice, it is almost a truism that the chief military worry of a Western army for the past 2,500 years was another Western army.'

Hanson's book is an extraordinary read and reminds us that European values had their darker side when applied to military organisation. Since 1945, however, the main thrust of the historiography on 'the Rise of the West'—the title of the Chicago historian William H. Mc Neill's best-selling, 828- page tome of 1963— has been to understand how the data summarised by Schuker can be explained. The significance of that data—the spectacular rise in growth and income of the West compared to Asian empires—Ottoman, Moghul and Chinese—which Schuker called 'the greatest achievement in the history of mankind' has given rise to a huge literature and caused the birth of a new school of historiography called 'global history'. Indeed, Daniel Chirot of the University of Washington begins his essay on the 'The Rise of the West' in Volume 50 (1985), No. 2, pp. 181-195 of the *American Sociological Review*, with the words: 'The most important question historical sociology can ask today as in the past century and a half is: Why did the West take such an enormous economic and technological lead over the rest of the world?' His answers are fairly typical of the huge number of books now available on the subject and of the kind that irritate the Dutch historian from the University of Leiden, P.H. H. Vries. The latter, in an exceedingly long article in Volume 30, No. 1 (Spring 2002), pp. 67-138 of the *Journal of World History* entitled 'Governing Growth: A Comparative Analysis of the Role of the State in the Rise of the West' responds to Chirot's question as follows: 'Almost every text on the subject refers to the peculiarity of Western Europe's states. To be more precise two related points have become stock in trade in the literature on the European miracle. Firstly, Europe was a system of states, not an empire, as was the rule in other advanced societies in the world. Secondly, states in Western Europe, as political entities were structured and governed differently from empires in the rest of the world, to a large extent because they were part of a system of states. The facts, of course, are undeniable.' He continues: 'Although it is not always said so explicitly, even a fairly superficial reading of the pertinent texts shows that the underlying explanatory mechanism their authors have in mind is competition. It is the constant competitive tension in the European state-system *between* European states as well as inside them that is presented as the motor of Europe's growth and the source of its dynamism.' Vries, himself, thinks that this explanation smacks of neo-Darwinism and neo-classical economics. It turns out that he prefers empires to states. They offer such economies of scale. He even speculates (pp. 80-81) on how European imperialism could have been improved by European unity: 'How much more could have been gained if the Europeans had sailed out as one Europe, united, incorporated, instead of as a pack of irreconcilable fighters?'

He is thus a 'good European' and perhaps should be given a job in Brussels. His long article rather disappointingly ends by attributing Europe's rise to the Industrial Revolution.—'...the great divergence arose with and because of the Industrial Revolution...The Industrial Revolution was a great divide in Western economic history and in the economic history of the entire globe.' (p. 126). The role of the state in the process of industrialization, therefore, is all that matters to him. The previous millennium is irrelevant.

Clearly, to do the historiography of 'the Rise of the West' true justice, I would need to examine the comparative histories of Europe, China, the Moghul and Ottoman Empires. MacNeill in his book started with pre-history and did indeed cover these non-European parts of the world. However, this is not a history textbook and, even if it were, I have neither the time nor space to write a history of the world. What I would like to do, briefly, in order to conclude this chapter, is simply to look at 'the European Miracle' and explain the points about the European state system, which to Vries's annoyance, do indeed occupy the attention and respect of nearly everyone who writes on the subject.

The best book on the topic is by the Australian economic historian Eric Jones and is now in its third edition. Indeed the 2003 edition by Cambridge University Press includes an 'afterword to the third edition' which engages with the wider historiography. The full title of the book is *The European Miracle. Environments, Economics and Geopolitics in the History of Europe and Asia*. For our purposes the two most important chapters are chapters six and seven, the first entitled 'the states system' and the second, 'nation-states'. The first is headed by a quotation from the American political scientist, Robert Wesson, the author of a book entitled *State Systems: International Pluralism, Politics and Culture* which asserts: 'That Europe maintained itself in a stable state of division for so many centuries of unexampled progress is historically miraculous'. Jones then takes up the story by arguing that Europe, in contrast to China, India or the Ottoman conquests, never became united as an empire, and instead became a system of states. In short, at the heart of the European miracle was not European unity but European disunity. He stresses that 'this is as crucial to understanding long-run economic development as it is to explaining the pattern of the industrial world that emerged in the nineteenth century.' He then demonstrates how a number of core agricultural areas became the bases for a number of competing states which through alliances within and without Europe (France allying with the Turks against the Habsburgs for example) used the balance of power to cement their independence. Indeed, the balance of power, (so demonised by European federalist politicians), he writes, is at the basis of the miracle: 'What shimmers in those depths is the miraculous preservation of the balance of power.' He agrees that the long-lasting nature of the system was miraculous since the checks and balances of the system—even the system of international law that it developed, were poor defences against the solid power of empires. Yet it had the advantage that long-lasting erroneous decisions could not be imposed on all states by some central imperial power—in contrast, for example, with the decision of the Ming court in 1480 not to have Chinese maritime exploration re-opened. The closest European parallel he can think of was the Pope's decision to divide the globe into Spanish and Portuguese spheres of influence—but the French simply ignored it. (There was no such clause in Adam's will, declared the King of France.)

Europeans, however, still considered themselves culturally connected despite their political divisions. They simply copied best practice. For example, between 1522 when Venice adopted 1 January as the first day of the year and

1752 when England did so, most of Europe, including Russia fell into line. Between 1582 when Spain, Portugal, France and the Italian states adopted the Gregorian calendar and 1752 when Britain did so eventually, that innovation was also accepted. (Russia, it is true, waited till 1918 to adopt it.) Religious unity, however, broke down in Europe very early but the eventual outcome in Western Europe of a split between Protestants and Catholics prevented either the imposition of a single politico-religious order (such as Confucianism in China) or an infinite splintering of beliefs. The result —quite fortuitously-- was a mixture of some Christian fraternity along with some freedom of thought. Diplomacy also served as reasonable cement. Latin and then French bound diplomats together and various treaties helped keep the peace. It was remarkable for example that during the Thirty Years War, English neutrality and trade were respected by the belligerents. French became the language of the aristocracy everywhere from the seventeenth century while Latin continued to be used by scholars and students who continued to travel around European universities without the need for travel documents even in countries at war. Meanwhile scientific discoveries and fashionable tastes in dress and furniture spread around Europe as princes, scientists and merchants visited different countries and observed innovations. Peter the Great went on his famous embassy around Europe to modernise Russia; Frederick and Catherine the Great invited the leading thinkers of their day to reside at their courts; there was also the Grand Tour by which aristocrats and the more highly educated and wealthy bourgeoisie could take the measure of European civilization. Later on industrial espionage was used to convey commercial secrets from one country to another, but before then, over centuries, rulers of one state would advertise for and recruit artisans, peasants and soldiers from others. Indeed, there were sometimes considerable movements of populations—Jews in the Middle Ages after their expulsion from a number of kingdoms, Huguenots, who after their expulsion from France in 1685 went to Prussia and England. All sorts of refugees fled the Turkish conquests in Eastern and Southern Europe, so that there was considerable movement around Europe whose states thus gained the advantages of being able to attract the best manufactures and manufacturers while retaining their own political habits and customs and safeguarding themselves from imperial conquest and centralization. Politically, too, there was a great deal of international observation. Voltaire and others visited England to inspect its constitution. Academies sprang up throughout Europe in the seventeenth and eighteenth centuries devoted to corresponding about and promoting enlightenment in government, economics and science by examining the most recent advances made in neighbouring countries. In the late nineteenth century Britain and other countries paid great attention to Bismarck's welfare reforms in Germany to see how much could be incorporated in domestic legislation. All sorts of learned journals reported on cultural, scientific and political developments abroad and educated Englishmen regularly read works in German. Keynes in his *Economic Consequences of the Peace* waxed eloquent on the international nature of the European state system before 1914 which still did not demand passports or visas for travel or study abroad. The First World War, he maintained, had not been expected by anybody.

It is true, of course, that throughout the centuries before 1914 the very need to safeguard their independence had meant that Europe's states were also extremely keen to acquire the latest and most efficient techniques in producing armaments, organising armies and raising revenues, all of which in turn helped promote economic growth. And, true, there were sometimes wars. Indeed, quite paradoxically, by the end of the eighteenth century some

Europeans believed that so much economic progress had been made that war in Europe would come to an end. Joseph Priestly, for example, wrote in 1792 that recent commercial treaties between England and France would bring permanent peace, while, later on Cobden and Bright and the 'Manchester School' again predicted that international trade would bring an end to war. Unfortunately the French Revolution and Napoleon and later on the Kaiser and Hitler gave the lie to this theory. However, between 1815 and 1914 peace in Europe did seem to be normal, although the opposition to the emergence of nation states on the part of the Habsburg and Ottoman Empires plus Prussia's desire to form a *Reich* or Empire (incorporating French, Danish and Polish as well as German territory) meant that an entirely peaceful community of nation states never quite came into being. The real challenge to peace became the desire for world empire—the Kaiser's famous *Griff nach der Weltmacht* or 'bid for world power' in Fritz Fischer's famous phrase, Hitler's attempt to build a global new order based on race, and communism's drive to deliver the world to a dictatorship of the proletariat through a series of revolutions. Peace and democracy, on the other hand, always remained the aims of Europe's nation states and today they have their best chance of achieving these goals not through the construction of an artificial, unhistorical and unnecessary European super-state or empire, but through mutual cooperation, free trade and membership of NATO, all of these things supporting a state system which would retain the best of that successful centuries' old tradition, which helped give rise to the European Miracle in the first place.

Indeed, the model of competing, independent states as the engine of progress in Europe can be shown to have persisted even after 1945. It is now known that it was not the European Union that caused economic growth after the war but the policies of individual reformers in different European states. The EEC for decades after its foundation spent most of its meagre resources on agriculture and fisheries. It had no policies or programmes for economic growth. EEC tariff cuts made at most an extremely marginal contribution to Western European economic growth and in any case their effect cannot be differentiated from tariff cuts made by EFTA. Later on after the international shocks of the 1970s—the end of the Bretton Woods system in 1971 and the oil prices rises forced by OPEC in 1973 and 1979-- the EEC policy was defensive and aimed at preserving sunset industries (e.g. the Davignon Plan for steel) while after the 1980s, despite the hopes placed in the Single Market and the single currency, both foreseen in the Maastricht Treaty of 1992, growth entered a period of relative decline from decade to decade, right up to the present. Indeed, the introduction of the euro was an economic disaster for Europe. Meanwhile growth in Europe after 1945 was aided by the actions of supply-side reformers in individual states. The currency reform of 1948 introduced with others to West Germany by Ludwig Erhard kick-started the phenomenal post-war growth of West Germany and her Low Country neighbours. (The European Payments Union under the Marshall Plan and of the 1948 General Agreement on Tariffs and Trade (GATT) also contributed.) Then in 1960 the introduction of the Rueff Plan in France continued the process. To quote Professor Eichengreen's classic work on *The West European Economy since 1945*: 'An economy no longer saddled with controls and cartels responded energetically to the reforms of the Rueff Plan...On 1 January 1960, when the Rueff Plan came into effect, 90 per cent of all grade with European markets and 50 per cent of trade with the dollar zone were freed. The Plan tackled the country's chronic fiscal deficits by limiting public sector pay increases to 4 per cent, cutting subsidies from nationalized companies and eliminating pensions for able-bodies ex-servicemen. It addressed inflation inertia by abolishing index-linking except in the case of the minimum wage. Capital formation was encouraged by tax provisions allowing for the accelerated depreciation of fixed investment...and [it] scal[ed] back the protection afforded small farmers. The results were out-migration from agriculture, rising farm productivity, and elastic supplies of labor to industry.' Stimulated by a devaluation of the franc, French companies consolidated themselves to secure economies of scale in export markets. Gross fixed investment rose from 17 to 22 percent over the previous decade. The French car industry expanded faster than the Japanese. In short, Jacques Rueff, in the words of the most reliable of historians of the EU, Professor John Gillingham III, currently at Harvard University, was 'the Ludwig Erhard of France'. His policies were then copied in Italy and Scandinavia. Margaret Thatcher in Britain in the 1980s continued the process of large-scale, national supply-side reforms, cutting taxes, taming the trade unions, and cutting back the state but now adding the privatisation of nationalised industries to the mix. Thatcherism, in turn, was copied by governments all over Europe and the world. Finally, in 2003 Gerhard Schroeder again revitalised the German economy by introducing supply-side reforms. In short, despite the existence of the EEC/EU, economic growth in Western Europe since the war has been caused by the traditional model of independent states introducing (supply-side) reforms and other independent states copying them. The EEC/EU with its dependence on centralised regulations and directives emanating from Brussels has always been irrelevant when not actually detrimental to the production of growth in Europe. The introduction of the single currency is undoubtedly the best example. The model of competing individual states gets validated in all sorts of contexts. For example, Fraser Nelson, the editor of the *Spectator* writing an article on how 'Immigration has brought tragedy to the world's most open country' in the *Daily Telegraph* on 13 November 2015, had this to say of the country in question, namely Sweden: 'Sweden seemed to be a lodestar to the world. George W. Bush had copied its pension policy, Tony Blair borrowed its hospitals policy, the Tories aped the free schools. It was the most socialistic country in the free world –yet still so entrepreneurial that it could sell cider to the English.' This is how progress really occurs.

Europe is a state system, not a state. Its progress had depended on its disunity, not its unity. Its states have made progress over centuries by copying and adapting institutions, policies, philosophies and practices found in neighbouring states. This is what was at the basis of the 'European Miracle' and should remain the case.

Such a system would also enable Britain to remain British, France to remain French, Germany to remain German, Italy to remain Italian etc. etc. and would spare us the incubus of a stumbling new European empire producing all-powerful bureaucrats and plastic Europeans. It would spare Europe an inevitable descent down the path of centralization with countries being overruled on their essential national interests, seeing their national traditions trampled on or seeing their national preferences disregarded by a federal bureaucracy issuing unchallengeable supranational legislation. It would avoid small countries being told when to open or close their borders, which economic policies to adopt and when, which technocrats to accept as prime ministers, or (soon enough) how to recruit regiments for a new European army to follow a foreign policy which might very well contradict their own national interests.

Accepting a new European Empire (or wannabbee super-state) might massage the egos of 'Good Europeans'; resisting it will inevitably prompt accusations of being 'Bad Europeans' against those devoted to maintaining the national sovereignty of democratic nation-states. In fact, resisting the imperial path—which will lead to lower standards of living and a loss of independence—should make such people, not 'Bad Europeans' but 'Better Europeans—indeed, the very best of Europeans. The European Miracle was caused, as has been seen, by Europe's survival for centuries as a state system. By remaining true to this heritage, by cooperating with one another just as European states did over the centuries, by establishing free trade and negotiating a reasonable degree of free movement of people, goods and capital and retaining a mutual defence through NATO, Europe can once again have a miraculous future. The European Miracle can continue. Federalists always claim that this alternative future would mean a return to the balance of power and war. When I took part in a debate in the Oxford Union a few years ago Will Hutton, now master of an Oxford college, claimed it would cause 'blood in the streets'. Really? Can anyone truly believe that the reinvigoration of EFTA would cause mass murder? Some have argued, on the other hand, that the EU already has blood on its hands by sparking off the Bosnian War and provoking civil war in Ukraine. These, however, are not my arguments. My own response would simply be to point out that most European states today have become so pacifist and have so thoroughly disarmed, that war among them would be technically impossible in any case. Most readers, however, will recognise that the argument that one or several member states withdrawing from the EU will lead to war, is unconvincing.

Brexit should be seen not as a step backward but as a positive step forward leading to that better Europe which the nightmare of European nationalism/federalism/imperialism—whatever you call it-- now subverts. Britain's exit from the EU should provide the opportunity for Europe to abandon 'ever-closer union' once and for all in favour of a vision of freely but closely cooperating, self-confident, democratic, sovereign states copying the best practices and advances of one another in all fields of human endeavour, but no longer subject to the diktats of overpaid, unaccountable bureaucrats in Brussels. This is a vision of a Europe of free peoples exploiting their cultural individualities and diversities but released from the failed experiment of European federalism with its bureaucratic centralism, lack of democratic accountability and its dream of becoming a future empire.

Chapter Two: Britain

Part One

The most successful of the states that constituted the European state system was undoubtedly Great Britain. Europhiles and Scottish Nationalists may wish to deny this, yet the truth is glaringly obvious. Admitting it would mean conceding that there is no need for Britain to be a member state of the EU or for Scotland to secede from the United Kingdom.

British history differs from that of other European countries in important ways. The British after all are not simply Europeans who speak English; nor are they merely a number of people who happen to inhabit the British Isles. They are the product of a peculiar national culture, which, in turn, is the creation of particular intellectual, environmental, social, geographical, political , economic, and institutional influences, all of which, have been historically determined. Perhaps the most important elements that have shaped the British national consciousness have been, first, government based on the rule of law through Parliament as the protector of individual liberty; secondly, political and social cohesion; and thirdly, world power. It is the combination of these three factors since the beginning of the eighteenth century which has made British history unique. So let us examine them in turn.

It was in the seventeenth century that the British pattern of government first diverged markedly from that of the rest of Europe. (I am following the historian E.N. Williams here.) This happened because the crown in England—I shall deal with Scotland and Ireland later—combined both strengths and weaknesses. Regarding the latter, its power over the citizen was limited by the common law. Agents of the executive could be tried in ordinary courts for deeds carried out in the course of their duties. Indeed, the chief agents of the crown could be arraigned before the highest court in the land, Parliament, as Charles I's minister, Strafford, was in 1641. The writ of *habeas corpus*, which ordered prison governors to produce a prisoner for regular trial, protected ordinary citizens from arbitrary arrest. Monarchs naturally attempted to frustrate such proceedings but ultimately failed to do so. Thus Charles II, for example, was foiled in his legal attack on his almost revolutionary opponent Lord Shaftesbury, by the actions of the Grand Jury of Middlesex which decided that Shaftesbury had no case to answer, thus saving his life. The rule of law, as a result, was upheld. Three factors, in retrospect, ensured this: first, the reverence which surrounded the supposedly immemorial traditions on which the rule of law was based; second, the tenacity with which it was defended by the common lawyers and the courts; but most important of all was the protection afforded to the rule of law by Parliament.

The High Court of Parliament was the second of the chief sources of weakness of the English monarchy. It consisted of the king, the House of Lords and the House of Commons, membership of which latter body was based on some form of election. By the seventeenth century Parliament as the highest court of justice and in addition was *alone* capable of changing the law or authorising taxation. More than that, it was claiming to tell the king which ministers he should appoint and which policies he should pursue. It went so far as to wage war on Charles I, defeat him and execute him. By 1650, therefore, this embodiment of the judiciary and legislature had become more than a check on the executive; it had become the executive itself.

The scale of Parliament's success seems very remarkable indeed compared with the fate of the Estates in most other European countries. There, continental monarchs were either eliminating their powers or putting an end to their existence altogether. At most they were stagnating in passive reaction. There is not room here to explain in any detail why the story had a different outcome in England, yet two factors were of the greatest importance. First, the Tudors used Parliament to make, unmake and then remake the English Reformation while, secondly, the economic and social changes of the sixteenth century enormously increased the wealth and pretensions of the classes who sat in Parliament.

There was another factor, however, that was also important in the rise of Parliament: the comparative smallness of the royal establishment. Few monarchies disposed of a smaller revenue than England in the sixteenth and seventeenth centuries and the same was true of the bureaucracy since the administration of local government and courts of justice was carried out by unpaid local officials. Indeed, even in the nineteenth century, with the development of Factory Acts and Poor Law Acts, British administration remained extraordinarily small by continental standards and as late as 1855 there were only 18,000 civil servants, including postmen. In 1910 a French author estimated that for every 10,000 inhabitants, Belgium had 200 officials, France 176, Germany 126, and Great Britain 73. Parliament, as a result, could never be intimidated or even bypassed by a royal bureaucracy. Most important of all in this respect was the fact that the king did not dispose of a large standing army. Englishmen rightly regarded a standing army as the greatest threat to their liberties. The example of Louis XIV, the Prussian kings, Napoleon, not to mention the military dictatorship of Oliver Cromwell himself, proved that armed forces had to be controlled. After the expulsion of James II in 1688 Parliament decreed that revenue for military purposes would have to be raised annually through the Army Act. The result was that in 1745 Bonnie Prince Charlie could reach Derby unopposed at the head of Highland clansmen and that in 1744 only 9,000 troops could be found to defend the country. True, huge armies could be raised in order to defeat Napoleon. But these were soon reduced in size once the war had been won and militarism was never to be a problem for Great Britain. By 1846, Wellington was once again reporting that only about 10,000 troops were available to defend the country and between 1873 and 1897 the army was unable to hold manoeuvres because Parliament refused to grant it money. Significantly, Great Britain did not create a general staff until the twentieth century.

Britain was even wary about creating an unbeatable navy. In the seventeenth century the Dutch navy was bigger than its British counterpart while in the eighteenth century a combination of French and Spanish fleets could be critical for Britain's imperial defence, as the American War of independence showed. In the nineteenth century the British fleet was cut down drastically from 214 commissioned ships of the line in 1815 to 68 in 1822 and 58 in 1835. It was the German decision to launch a naval race at the very end of the nineteenth century that finally made the British Parliament keener to spend money on the fleet in peacetime. Thus from the seventeenth to the twentieth centuries, Parliament's refusal to spend money on a standing army or even a sea-ready navy seriously undermined the power of the British executive.

Yet how was this tradition of a small bureaucracy and few armed forces able to take root so firmly in British soil? To some extent the answer is geographical. The surrounding seas had long provided England with excellent internal communication, with the result that unification was achieved very early. The same waters also protected England from foreign invasion. Unlike many a continental state, therefore, England was not in danger of falling apart into sub-regions or provinces or of being cut in pieces by a powerful neighbour. Almost as a piece of luck, she could afford the luxury of being lightly administered, so that while 'Continental states could not survive outside the iron lung of absolute rule, Englishmen could stretch themselves under a bureaucratic framework as light as gossamer.'

The final victory of Parliament was established by a series of enactments at the turn of the seventeenth and eighteenth centuries, the expulsion of James II and William III's wars against Louis XIV, having enormously strengthened Parliament's authority. By the end of the reign of Queen Anne, therefore, it had been established that the crown would remain in Protestant hands so that absolutism and divine right should no longer trouble Britain; that judges should be placed entirely outside the reach of the executive and accused persons granted more safeguards; that the king could not raise an army without parliamentary consent; that censorship of the press should end; that Parliament should meet regularly and often (defined as at least every three years, leading to twelve elections between 169 and 1715); that religious toleration should be extended; and that only a very small part of the crown's total needs should be granted for life. The rest was to be voted and audited by act of parliament, it being taken for granted as a general maxim, in the words of Bishop Barnet, that a revenue for a certain and a short time was the best security that the nation could have for frequent parliaments.

While other European countries, therefore, were experiencing the age of absolutism or enlightened despotism, Great Britain was establishing parliamentary government. Paradoxically, moreover, this proved a stronger system than absolutism, despite the fact that Britain had no standing army or (before the eighteenth century) great navy. First, national unity had been established early; England, moreover, was a judicial area with a uniform system of law. To an increasing extent she was also an economic unit; what obstacles there were to the growth of a national market were physical ones erected by nature, not custom posts set up by privileged sub-units. Economic growth had been fostered by a strong Tudor state which had suppressed banditry, defied foreign power and turned the Church into a national one, the Church of England. All this meant that the nation was united to a degree unknown among the Continental states and that nationalism appeared in England (and soon Britain) before it developed elsewhere. This sense of unity in turn became extraordinarily powerful when articulated by a Parliament that represented the nation. And this is what was happening by the end of the seventeenth century. Parliament, populated by the same elites who, as lords lieutenants and justices of the peace, ran local government and who provided a sufficient electorate to make elections meaningful, was able to mobilise the country. All that remained was for the House of Commons to become increasingly representative, something that was to happen through the Reform Acts of 1832, 1867 and 1884 and the grant of the vote to women. Thus the first distinguishing feature of modern British history can be said to be the experience of continuous parliamentary government based on the rule of law—as opposed to absolutist, bureaucratic or militaristic government—over the course of three centuries.

The second distinguishing feature of British history is undoubtedly the political and social cohesion enjoyed by Britons during the same period. There have of course been moments of political and social tension during these centuries—one thinks of 1745, the 1790s, 1839, 1848—but these do not appear too serious in comparison with events experienced elsewhere. In modern times Britain has witnessed no political revolutions, no foreign invasions, no occupations, and no dictatorships of left or right, or even any significant support for fascist or communist doctrines. No minorities have been deliberately persecuted and the rule of law has never been put aside for political reasons. This is a singular record for a European country.

In many ways this is the direct result of the early establishment of parliamentary government as well as the success of parliamentary reform. For Parliament, once reformed, proved susceptible to the demands of nineteenth- and twentieth century social reformers. There was little need for social critics to indulge in revolutionary action. It was also a consequence of religious radicalism. For the same religious non-conformism that challenged the absolutist pretensions of the Stuart dynasty in the seventeenth century, revived itself towards the end of the eighteenth century, led the movement to abolish the slave trade and slavery in the British Empire, and went on to champion social and political reform at home. This meant that socialism in Great Britain, for example, developed along different lines from Continental socialism, being always rooted in a religious and parliamentary soil. The Labour Party owed more to Methodism than to Marx, and there was something terribly British about Robert Owen's hopes for establishing 'harmony communities' and 'co-operatives'. He was in fact attempting to make social reform non-partisan. However, if such reform could not help but be a political issue, the fact that the British Parliament was not a bourgeois sham and that all parties—another result of the early establishment of parliamentarianism in Great Britain—were willing to tackle social reform meant that it was not until the beginning of the twentieth century that the Labour Party was formed as a separate vehicle for social advance. And even then, right up till the First World War, the Labour Party could still be regarded as a pressure group within the Liberal Party. This fact—the lack of a separate socialist party operating within the framework of the world's oldest parliamentary system—before the First World War—is itself a striking testimony to the political and social cohesion enjoyed by the British people.

It was proof, one might say, of the essentially pragmatic, unideological and moderate consensus which underlay British politics. Attlee himself guaranteed that the Labour Party would abide by this consensus when he wrote in the introduction to a three-volume, official history of the Labour Party in 1948, that it was a 'characteristically British production differing widely from Continental Socialist Parties' and 'a product of its environment and of the national habit of mind.'

If British socialism, therefore, was shaped in a moderate mould, so, too, was British right-wing politics. The reason for this was that national unity was never really questioned. The country had no significant linguistic minorities. True, Welsh was spoken in the North of Wales, and in the Scottish Highlands some Gaelic survived, but Welsh nationalism was never a problem after the Tudors, and Scotland was spectacularly absorbed into the Union, after a rough start, with no obvious grievances until almost the twenty-first century. Even the Irish Question was treated with much moderation.

As far as Scotland was concerned, the Scots were allowed to keep their own system of law (contrast that with the imposition of European law above Scottish law under the EU), their own system of education, and their own

Church. They were represented in both houses of Parliament and provided prime ministers and cabinet ministers. They more or less ran the British Empire—or so it often seemed—with the result that they had very few causes for complaint. What grievances they had were mollified when a Secretary of State for Scotland was created in 1885 and a Home Rule bill was given a second reading in 1913. Had the First World War not broken out in 1914, it is probable that Scotland would have received self-government that year.

Ireland, of course, was a completely different problem. It had a predominantly Catholic population, was ruled by foreign landlords and a foreign Church and lacked self-government during the nineteenth century. On the other hand, it was strategically vital to Britain's defences. Yet, it is a travesty of history to see the British record in Ireland as one of systematic repression. Governments throughout the nineteenth century devoted themselves to reform there, disestablishing the Church of Ireland, pushing through land reforms, protecting tenants, and attempting to secure Home Rule. Gladstone, it will be remembered, attempted no less than four times to put a Home Rule Bill on the statute book. Nor should it be forgotten that Irish MPs played a notable part in the history of the House of Commons during the battles to pass these bills. Still, it was left to Lloyd George in 1921 to settle the main problem, although even then he had to leave the Ulster problem unresolved. On the other hand, it simply cannot be denied that the majority of the population of Ulster felt and still feel passionately British and have no desire to become part of a united Ireland.

So much then for political cohesion. Social cohesion has also been a feature of British life and once more to a remarkable degree, since, if Britain experienced no violent political changes after 1688, she experienced no social ones either. Thus William III's much maligned 'Dutch money men'—camp followers who had come over from Holland after the Glorious Revolution--were easily absorbed at the beginning of the eighteenth century and the British aristocracy and gentry were able to maintain their social ascendancy right up till the twentieth century. That they were able to do so was the consequence of a number of important factors, all of them having to do with the different ways in which they channelled their social influence. They did this, for example, through their prestige in political affairs, through the extent of their landholdings, through their control of local administration, not to mention through the survival of popular deference. Two other factors, however, were of importance: the willingness of the aristocracy to accept key political and social reforms, and the fact that they in no way constituted a rigid political caste. The House of Lords, it should be remembered, had no fixed membership and could, as a result, absorb political rivals from the professional classes and business worlds within its ranks.

By the twentieth century the aristocracy no longer dominated social or political life. The middle and upper classes did that. On the other hand, the working class was now also much better organised   and in 1923 the Labour Party came to power. Yet even in the twentieth century Great Britain saw a huge degree of political and social cohesion thanks to the strength of the parliamentary tradition and of the steady rise in living standards. For example, even in the 1930s people were for the most part becoming better off. More houses were being built then than are being built today. The rub, of course, was that between the two world wars two to three million Britons were unemployed. Yet that is now seen as only part of the picture and the dismal decade is no longer seen as dismal any more. In the words of one historian, 'most English people were enjoying a richer life than any previously known in the history of the world: longer holidays, shorter hours, higher real wages. They had motor cars, cinema, radio sets, electrical appliances.' In the words of another: 'we may need to look beyond the critics and recognise the significance of a decade which saw for many the beginnings of affluence, the evolution of the welfare state and a confirmation of the stability of British politics.' In the light of such statements, it is easy to see why fascism was a non-starter in Britain in the 1930s. The success of the Nazis and Fascists in Europe lay in the insecurities of the German and Italian middle and lower-middle classes. Yet the British middle classes were anything but insecure after 1931 with the return of the National Government with a 500-seat majority, the rout of the Labour party, which in any case clearly had no idea what to do about the depression, and the maintenance of a reasonably stable if not improving standard of living. Nor did the workers present a threat. In 1935 only 18,000 people voted communist. In George Orwell's words: 'Between 1931 and 194, the National Government represented the will of the mass of the people.' This kind of situation was to repeat itself in the 1980s and 1990s, when, despite, recessions and massive increases in unemployment to the same levels as in the 1930s, Labour again proved incapable of winning elections since those in work experienced tangible improvements in the standards of living.

It was World war Two, however, that saw British political and social cohesion reach its peak and, given the post-war implementation of the Beveridge Report and the foundation of the welfare state through the establishment of the National Health Service and other institutions, this cohesion survived the war. The welfare state was accepted by all the political parties and full employment was taken as the common aim. The nation, in fact, had become a Keynesian democracy with an accepted list of social priorities. The new consensus was christened 'Butskellism' by the *Economist* from the names of the Labour and Conservative Chancellors, Hugh Gaitskell and R.A. Butler. Everybody knew instinctively what this epithet signified, namely that there was no discernible difference between the two major political parties. This had also been the moral of a novel, *Gentian Violet*, published in 1953 by Edward Hyams in which the hero managed to get elected to Parliament as both a Socialist and a Tory without anybody noticing the difference.

This post-war consensus lasted till the 1980s when Margaret Thatcher's premiership bitterly divided the country. The trades unions were reformed, almost all nationalized industries were privatised and taxes were cut. Her victory over the miners and the attempted introduction of a poll tax caused not merely great resentment but riots. Yet her political overthrow in 1990 led merely to another Tory majority and it was not until 1997 that Tony Blair could Labour to power. Significantly he talked of 'New Labour', dropped Clause Four of the 1918 Labour Party constitution which called for the nationalisation of industry, and instituted a strategy of 'triangulation' which meant adopting Tory political values. In short, Thatcher had, whatever her initial impact, initiated a new political consensus more sensitive to the needs of private enterprise and the role of competition in industry.

The post-war consensus also attached to foreign policy, for in the era of the Cold War, the British had no doubts about which side they were on. The resulting inter-party agreement could, therefore, be satirised in the following verse:

'The Bevin or the Churchill touch
Seem both alike to Danes and Dutch.
If Socialist or Tory speaks,
It's all the same to French and Greeks.'

Without doubt the vast majority of Britons believed that with the creation of the welfare state, the achievement of full employment, and the experience of rising standards of living, their system of parliamentary democracy constituted a socio-political system which communism, like fascism, could only threaten but never rival.

With the Bevin and the Churchill touch we come to the last of the three broad distinguishing traits of modern British history, namely Britain's role as a world power. This was based first, on the creation of the Empire, secondly on Britain's leadership in the first Industrial Revolution, thirdly on Britain's dominance of world financial markets, and finally, on Britain's success in innumerable wars. There is no need to discuss the origins of the Industrial Revolution, but one of its results was that the wealth of the country plus the wealth of the City money markets enabled Great Britain to wage war when necessary, with the consequence that she could finance the wars against Napoleon, take on the supposed military might of Russia in 1854 and survive two world wars victoriously. Yet Britain's position as the world's financial centre really predated the Industrial Revolution and went back to the foundation of the Bank of England in 1694, the creation of the National Debt in 1693 and the re-coinage of 1696. These measures together with the evolution of an effective system of tax-collection during the eighteenth century meant that British governments were in an extremely strong position regarding international credit. Once again the parliamentary system played a role. The fact that the commercial and trading elites as well as the landed ones were represented in Parliament meant that governments could borrow money in anticipation of revenue, since these elites had confidence that the monies borrowed would be properly collected, controlled and repaid. Hence at many stages of the eighteenth and nineteenth centuries, Britain was the only great power which really could afford a war, something which, however, she tried to avoid.

In the nineteenth century Britain found excuses for remaining free of European entanglements—imperial problems, no clear government majority, refusal to commit future parliaments, etc. Her wise policy was to pursue only her own best interests by means of free hands (no alliances or other commitments if they could be avoided) and free trade. Among many others Bismarck ridiculed her refusal to come to terms ('I wasted five years of my life in the belief that England was a great power'), yet Britain's only alliance was with Japan in 1902 (with the *casus foederis* dependent on attack by *two* other powers). She meanwhile patiently negotiated *ententes*, increased her defence expenditure and cut her commitments. In this way she avoided European wars right up to 1914, when Europe's supra-national Habsburg Monarchy deliberately started a war which it knew might well engulf the whole of Europe, a probability which was made a certainty when the small state of Belgium was invaded by the troops of the supra-national German Empire on their way to conquer France.

Only in 1955, given the threat posed by a new supra-nationalist ideology, Communism (Nazism and Fascism having been defeated in World War Two) did Britain agree to station an army abroad in peacetime by creating the British Army of the Rhine This helped bring about the consolidation of NATO, whose ever-formidable existence played a major part in ending the Soviet Union in 1991.

Let us now examine the significance in British history of the British Empire. It came about in piece-meal fashion and from a variety of motives. The eighteenth century empire was the result primarily of economic rapacity, although religion and geographical curiosity were also involved. Large parts of India and North America were seized from other European powers or native rulers. The abomination of the slave trade was a major economic factor. However, this amazing piece of institutionalised international plunder collapsed in the West in 1776 with the American Declaration of Independence and the ensuing war.

The nineteenth-century empire was different. Plunder still went on, but on a much reduced scale. Slavery was abolished and the evangelical revival brought a revolution in public ethics. Moreover, the American War had taught rationally-minded men that all colonies would one day have to be granted independence. Thus Macaulay, for example, could tell the House of Commons in 1833 during a debate on the India Bill of that year: 'The public mind of India, having become instructed in European knowledge…may in some future age demand European institutions. Whether such a day will ever come, I know not. But never will I attempt to retard it. Whenever it comes, it will be the proudest day in English history.' Between the 1830s and 1850s an attempt was made to start the process of educating Indians towards eventual self-rule. The Indian Mutiny of 1857, it is true, completely altered the position and thereafter India was run by the British, paying for its own defence and partly subsidising British defences. The British, however, paid for major works of infrastructure. Whether Britain made a profit out of India is difficult to say, but if she did, this was the exception in colonial history, not the rule.

The truth is that for most of the nineteenth century, the British did not want an empire, certainly not in the formal sense. Colonies lost money and even Disraeli referred to them as 'millstones around our necks'. Colonies had to be defended, administered and controlled. Nine times out of ten they provided little in the way of markets and often involved unnecessary wars. British governments, therefore, avoided picking them up when possible (the exceptions being ocean coaling-stations.) Where possible white colonies were granted self-government. None the less, the expansion of empire had not yet reached an end. For towards the end of the nineteenth century, European imperialism, now reinforced by the rising spectre of commercial protectionism, forced Britain once again to expand her formal empire. The process, it should be pointed out, had nothing to do with the export of capital, as critics of the Left maintained. Lenin, for example, obviously did not understand what had happened when he wrote his book on imperialism. The facts were that only 2-5% of Europe's capital exports went into the new colonies. Most British overseas investment went into independent states, particularly America but also Argentina and Peru. There was also much European investment in China, which, unlike Africa, was not partitioned. Moreover, many of the states with empires—Italy, Russia, Spain, Portugal and the USA—were themselves importers of capital. Nor did European powers feel compelled to go to war with one another over colonies because of investments. The Germans and French put more money into British colonies than their own; indeed, it was almost impossible for German governments to get German businessmen to invest in newly acquired deserts and swamps—far less to persuade German colonists to go there in significant numbers. Decolonization, not illogically therefore, brought increased economic growth. Nor was it necessary to pacify the new working class with the fruits of empire to stop them from revolting, as Marxist writers had implied. The European workers who had the highest standard of living were the Scandinavians and the Swiss—all citizens of states which lacked empires altogether.

Other points of misunderstanding can be cleared up as well. Britain, for example, never attempted —as did the French—to assimilate her colonial subjects. She never intended to make them British, but worked through local rulers—tribal chiefs, sheikhs and maharajas—to maintain public order and control. This explains why so very few troops or administrators were necessary to keep the empire going: it had the collaboration of the local elites. Eventually these began to demand self-government, which the British by the second half of the twentieth century were quite willing to grant. Until then, to quote Professor M.S Anderson:

'Nothing is more striking than the ease with which small, sometimes very small numbers of Europeans were able to transform the whole existence of large parts of the world. Apart from the Maratha and Sikh states few Indian principalities offered sustained resistance to the spread of British rule. When the nineteenth century ended the whole of the subcontinent, with a population already approaching 300 million, was controlled by an army which included only 70,000 white soldiers and of which a large part was stationed permanently on the Afghan frontier...Even in Egypt, where nationalism was rapidly gaining strength, a population which by 1900 approached 10 million was effectively controlled by a British army of occupation which sometimes numbered less than 5,000. Numerically most striking of all, in 1896 about 3 million people in southern Uganda were ruled by perhaps 25 British officials.

Professor Bernard Porter quotes one colonial governor in Kenya reporting before 1914 in the racist language of the time: 'Here we are three white men in the heart of Africa, with 20 Nigger soldiers and 50 Nigger police, 68 miles from doctors or reinforcements, administering and policing a district inhabited by half a million well-armed savages...the position is most humorous.' Hitler and Stalin could not believe how the British ran their empire.

Perhaps precisely because so few people were involved in running it and because most British emigrants went to the white dominions or the USA, the Empire never won much public support. The working classes were simply uninterested in it. In fact, it only meant something when large numbers were called upon to fight for it, as in the Boer War. Most of them thought that the money could be better spent on social reform at home. Joseph Chamberlain's programme of imperial preferences and Empire Development was perhaps not surprisingly defeated at the polls in 1906 by a huge majority. Even during World War One, H.G. Wells could write: 'nineteen people out of twenty, the lower class and most of the middle class knew no more of the Empire than of the Argentine republic or the Italian Renaissance. It did not concern them.'

After the war, many attempts were made to alter this situation through all sorts of organisations and press crusades. This made no difference, for the Chairman of the Empire Day Movement had to admit that 'in spite of unremitting efforts' there were 'still many dark corners in Great Britain, especially the industrial areas, where the rays of our Empire had simply failed to catch on. In 1948 a public opinion poll showed that three-quarters of the population did not know the difference between a dominion and a colony and that half could not name a single British colony. This was striking proof that the propaganda of the imperialists had secured an almost pathetic return.

By 1948, however, the post-war Labour government had already made a start on decolonisation. Churchill, who had declared during the war that he would never preside over the dissolution of the British Empire, lost the 1945 general election. The process of decolonisation then continued apace, in some places perhaps at too fast a pace. Certainly, independent Africa has witnessed much greater bloodshed, dictatorship and oppression since independence than before. The point to note is that however one judges Britain's imperial record, it has not affected British attitudes very much. Nobody wants the empire back; it was never a popular cause while it existed; it was ruled with the collaboration of native elites and when this collaboration stopped the colonies were quickly and usually very smoothly granted independence. Britain, unlike France, Portugal or even Holland, suffered no trauma over decolonisation. If the Commonwealth were to disappear tomorrow, very few people in Britain would even notice.

Foreigners never really understood that it was simply geography and not Empire which made Great Britain appear to be in many ways un-European. The very fact that Britain was an island with trading links all over the world gave Britain a different outlook from the Continental, land-based powers. Yet most of Britain's trade was with the USA and the Dominions, Germany and Latin America, not with her newly acquired colonies. The result was that the latter could very easily be given up. The final proof, therefore, that Empire was the least significant element in Britain's historical tradition, can be found in the smooth transition from Empire to Commonwealth. Britain after 1945 felt no obligation whatever to fight colonial wars to hang on to recalcitrant territories (strategic bases like Cyprus and Aden were a different matter). She did not experience the agony of an Algeria or of a slower war of attrition such as took place in Angola. Instead, supported by a populace which fundamentally adhered to the views of that Macaulay had put forward, she applied them to colonies all over the world as yet another part of the post-war consensus. The remarkable and not unflattering aspect of this process was that nearly every former colony involved demanded a British-type constitution and entered the Commonwealth. Indeed, even countries which had never been part of the Empire applied to join (e.g. Mozambique) and others that had left temporarily were glad to return (e.g. South Africa). This constituted an enormous political success and said much for British rule. So, too, does the fact that outside Europe, the world's most stable democracies—Canada, Australia, New Zealand, the United States, India—are all former British colonies.

Great Britain's history, therefore, has been unique. Britain experienced three centuries of continuous parliamentary government as well as social and political cohesion at a time when she was the world's leading power. All these factors were, as has been seen, inter-related. It might well be argued—if

Americans in particular will forgive me—that modern British history has been a success story without equal and that at the centre of that success story has been the maintenance of the rule of law by a democratic and sovereign Parliament. Today, however, Britain seems unaware of its historical success. The sovereignty of parliament and the rule of law have been delegated in key areas of public policy to the stumbling bureaucracy of the European Union. It is quite amazing that this should ever have happened.

One key reason why the British have accepted this is the myth of Britain's decline in the twentieth century. Historians like Professor Edgerton may have destroyed this myth but large sections of the worlds of journalism and politics cling on to it tenaciously, especially Europhiles who seem desperate to believe that EU membership saved Britain from decline and that outside the EU, an independent, self-governing Britain would once again be doomed. This is utter historical nonsense.

Part Two

The British still believed in their success right up till the 1960s. True, there were warning voices arguing that compared to, say, West Germany, we were experiencing less economic growth. Yet West German income levels did not surpass average British ones till the early 1960s; West Germany, moreover, had no nuclear weapons and no really functioning army till the mid-1960s and enjoyed no world role. France, meanwhile, had approached the verge of civil war over Algeria, had witnessed the fall of the Fourth Republic and the advent of de Gaulle and a new constitution. Yet de Gaulle in 1968 had had to flee his country amidst student revolts and widespread strikes; while in Greece the military had seized power thus adding another dictatorship in Western Europe to those of Spain and Portugal. The British therefore had reason enough to trust their institutions, whatever the critics had to say.

The political scandals of the 1960s (although quite trivial in retrospect), de Gaulle's veto of our first Common Market entry bid in 1963 (today his press conference statement seems entirely rational), and most of all, perhaps, the devaluation of the pound in 1967 (seen by many as a devaluation of our national status) led many political commentators to talk of our 'decline'. Many of them kept bringing up Suez as a turning point in international affairs, although, today, international historians accept that it was of very little significance. The 'special relationship' was patched up so quickly that within a couple of years the USA and Britain were landing troops almost simultaneously in Jordan and Lebanon in blatant continuation of great power intervention in the Middle East. Only a few years after that, in 1962, in the most spectacular demonstration of the continuation of the 'special relationship' between Britain and the USA, the Kennedy administration was selling Polaris missiles to Macmillan (one of the greatest advocates of Suez); and Britain would always remain the only country to which the USA would sell such weapons of mass destruction. Still, given our retreat from East of Suez after 1968, the failures of the Heath, Wilson and Callaghan governments in the 1960s and 1970s, the apparent dominance of the trades unions by communists, radicals, or merely blinkered old war-horses, many commentators began to write of 'Britain's decline'. Soon, there was a flood of books on the 'British disease' and for many people, Britain seemed to have become 'the sick man of Europe'. By 1979 there was almost no debate about this and Britain was represented as in its death throes. The economic historian Sidney Pollard, wrote in 1982: 'Britain is no longer counted among the economically advanced nations of the world. A wide gap separates her from the rest of industrialised Europe. The difference as measured in national product per head between Britain and, say, Germany, is now as wide as the difference between Britain and the continent of Africa.' The Europhile journalist Peter Jenkins, writing in the *Guardian* in September 1978, had been even more alarmist: 'No country has yet made the journey from developed to underdeveloped. Britain could be the first to embark upon that route.' Later on in the mid-1990s, after Britain's ejection from the Exchange Rate Mechanism in 1992 with subsequent economic problems such as the implosion of the housing market, (ejection from the ERM, of course, was accompanied by the revival of Eurosceptic demands for withdrawal from the EU altogether), Europhile defeatism of this kind was to resurrect itself. The ardent Europhile, Professor Stephen Haseler, was to write to the *Times* on 28 May 1996: 'The UK is too small to be independent—in the modern global economy a nation of 55 million is simply no longer able to determine its own economic policy or deal as an equal with international capital –and it is too big to enable the citizen to participate.' He had no advice for smaller nations. What were Canada, Australia and New Zealand supposed to do? They were hardly likely to be candidates for EU membership. Was the USA too big for its citizens to be able to participate in government? The Liberal Democrat MP, Paddy Ashdown, meanwhile, while calling on British troops to sacrifice themselves if necessary to defend the independence of Bosnia, could argue that any idea of Britain herself being independent was a delusion that only a 'xenophobe' or 'false patriot' could entertain, since it was impossible to be independent in an 'inter-dependent' world. On the other hand, he appeared to have nothing against the independence of Japan, Israel, Singapore, New Zealand, Canada or Australia. His argument was simply—*le mot juste*-- against British independence. In the *Sunday Times* of 4 August 1996, the novelist Robert Harris, another Europhile, wrote that the British should always remember the 'D-word'—decline. In his opinion, even after forty years, the memory of Suez and the catharsis that episode was supposed to represent, should be engraved on British minds. The Britishness of these people seemed to be limited to their desire to be good losers.

The solution to 'the British problem' that all these people had in mind was, of course, self-obliteration in 'Europe'. Thus writing in *Prospect* magazine in 1996, Simon Head expressed their common belief that whereas British diplomacy since 1945 had been an abject failure. French diplomacy during the same period, on the other hand, had served its country well. A little thought —a little knowledge of international history—might well, however, have produced a different judgement, yet since France had apparently tied her future to 'Europe', the false conclusion followed.

A true account of the relative diplomatic records of the two countries since 1945 would have been altogether more favourable to Britain. Immediately after the war, France was defeated over her German policy, was then defeated in Vietnam and defeated in Algeria, the latter debacle leading to the fall of the Fourth Republic. She was also defeated over the Saarland, over the European Defence Community (EDC) and over Suez (a French, not a British idea), while the founder of the Fifth Republic, General de Gaulle, was defeated on almost everything including the reorganization of NATO (he withdrew militarily from the whole organization), the Fouchet Plan, US nuclear aid, and his attempt to protect Eastern Europe from the USSR. Indeed, he even managed to get himself thrown out of Canada. Internationally, he was totally isolated, something which hardly served French interests very well. Americans regarded him as public enemy number one; the British thought of him as barmy; while France's European partners opposed almost his every move (The West German Bundestag emasculated the Franco-German Friendship Treaty of 1963 by attaching a pro-British and pro-NATO preamble to it. In 1966 the other members of the EEC refused to accept his views on the Common Market, leading to the Luxembourg Compromise which they refused to dignify with legal status.) The Soviets and Chinese had little time for him either despite his opposition to the war in Vietnam.

De Gaulle's successor Pompidou, achieved very little other than allowing Britain to enter the EEC in a vain attempt to control the Germans; otherwise his stated plans for the EEC got nowhere while his challenge to Henry Kissinger in 1973 over 'the year of Europe' and OPEC brought no gains for France. Giscard, the next French President, travelled a lot but achieved little of substance; eventually, the strange homage paid him by a cannibal African emperor (coronation arranged in Paris) made France look ridiculous, while his own regal pretensions (*le roi Giscard*) only added to that impression. As for Mitterrand, once the episode of 'socialism in one country' died a death, the main policy of this corrupt ex-fascist became subservience to Germany, whose re-unification, however, he did momentarily resist ('This means the outbreak of World War Three' was his first reaction). He then saddled France with the '*le franc fort*' as an economic policy which was otherwise known as rule from Frankfurt. He also signed the Maastricht Treaty which 49%of French voters opposed in what was widely regarded as a rigged plebiscite.

During the same period, the UK for its part decolonized successfully with no major hitches. She even won a war in Malaysia and took part in the defence of South Korea. In 1954 she stopped the Americans from using atom bombs in Vietnam in order to save Head's heroes, the French, at Dien Bien Phu. In Europe she saved Greece from Communism, helped establish the Council of Europe in 1949, and in the same year assisted in the creation of both NATO and the Federal Republic of Germany. She presided over the Geneva

Conference of 1954 which allowed the French to withdraw peacefully from Vietnam, and in 1955 she saved the day with regard to West German rearmament by agreeing to establish the British Army of the Rhine (BAOR) after France had scuttled the EDC. Despite the Suez fiasco, into which she had been led by the French, she quickly repaired her 'special relationship' with the USA and in 1958 cooperated with the Americans in in peacekeeping in the Middle East. In 1962 she used her influence to become the only country in the world to buy the latest nuclear weapons (Polaris missiles) from the USA and secured the right to use them independently. Later on she was to repeat this deal with Trident. She remained a stabilizing force East of Suez until 1973 and did not become involved in the Vietnam War despite heavy US pressure. In 1983 she won the Falklands War and by so doing did more for Latin American democracy in recent times than the USA, Fidel Castro and Che Guevara combined. She also negotiated a peaceful exit from Hong Kong, which secured its economic future as part of China, negotiated an end to the Rhodesian War and negotiated a peaceful end to the 'Irish Troubles'. When Saddam Hussein invaded Kuwait and war broke out in the Gulf in 1991, she became America's principal ally; the French defence minister meanwhile resigned and Germany, deliberately choosing to misinterpret its own constitution, refused to fight. True, Great Britain became a member state of the EU in 1973 and signed up to subsequent EU treaties, but despite this her diplomatic record was substantially more successful than that of the French during the period however reluctant Europhile commentators like Head might be to admit it. Yet the constant drip of criticism and the continuous deliberate downgrading of Britain's historical record meant that serious intellectual damage was done to the traditional self-confidence which the British educated public until the

1960s and 1970s had always retained about the country's (as we have seen) highly successful past.

The greatest damage was done, however, concerning the economic record. The statistics will be examined in a moment, but some general points have to be considered first. Critics continually asserted the low prestige of engineers in Britain, a bias in favour of the arts, banking, the civil service and the law. All this was supposed to cause decline. Usually Britain's educational and class systems were mixed into the argument—the classical education of the public schools, training for empire rather than industry, the lack of technical education etc.—all leading to the conclusion that Britain traditionally lacked entrepreneurial spirit and indeed was culturally conditioned to despise industry. Yet on most of the questions raised by these sorts of assertions almost no comparative work had been done. Did France and Germany have no class systems, no old-boy net-works, no elite educational institutions? Again, if empire had something to do with it, why did Germany and the United States who started obtaining colonies at the end of the nineteenth century not suffer economic decline as a result? The same point might be made about Japan. Again, if imperial values impede economic growth, how could France who was fighting two bitter colonial wars between 1945 and 1962 undergo an 'economic miracle' while 'declining' Britain was peacefully transforming Empire into Commonwealth? In any case, in the age of imperialism before 1914, growth in the British economy increased steadily, dipped slightly between 1900 and 1907 and then recovered by 1914.

One very influential work that reinforced the view that British traditional class structures and attitudes had brought about 'decline' was Martin Wiener's *English Culture and the Decline of the Industrial Spirit*, published in 1981 to great praise from reviewers. It argued that the British had been conditioned culturally to despise industry both by their men of letters and by their political and social elites. The trouble was that such 'history' of course is totally unscientific since even if it can be shown that many people disliked industry and the industrial process, it cannot be shown how this contributed in any way to Britain's 'decline'. Wiener seemed to argue that since economic historians had failed to substantiate this by economic explanations, cultural factors must necessarily carry conviction. His hypothesis also asserted that the bourgeois class of entrepreneurs who had made the industrial revolution had all become gentrified and absorbed into the upper classes with their values based on land. Germany and America were supposedly different. In Germany the bourgeois class had not been so absorbed and in the USA there was never any opposition to the industrial spirit.

Alas it simply was not true that only British men of letters disdained the industrial spirit. For example, one study of American literature discovered that in 'the entire body of American fiction...the businessman (was) almost always depicted as crass, philistine, corrupt, predatory, domineering, reactionary and amoral.' Only three business novels presented a positive side to him at all. According to the brilliant American political and intellectual historian, Richard Hofstadter, moreover, 'the agrarian myth' was not 'a popular but a literary idea' in America, 'a preoccupation of the upper classes, of those who enjoyed a classical education, read pastoral poetry, experimented with breeding stocks and owned plantations or country estates.' In Germany, too, the intellectuals shunned industrialism and Professor R. Hilton Thomas has written of a cultural gradation there 'with values derived from a society of a different order [that] acquired such an aura and authority that when the new industrial reality materialized towards the end of the nineteenth century, this was not easily absorbed into the intellectual context.' Writers such as Lagarde, Heym, Schlaf,

Tucholsky, and Kraus could as a result be quoted in the same way as Wiener quotes their English counterparts.

The real conclusion to be drawn is that industrialism was not particularly welcomed by intellectuals anywhere. This is not surprising. It is not an inherently likeable process and certainly not one which recommends itself to intellectuals who are irrelevant to it. In the wider context perhaps the last word should be left to Professor Fritz Stern:

'This anti-capitalist sentiment was of course endemic in the western world; its history has yet to be written and when it is, it most likely will reveal that this anti-capitalist mood sprang from nostalgia for a simple life of some lost Arcadia, but also from nostalgia for a religious faith that seemed doomed to extinction at the same time.'

Wiener was not merely very parochial in his treatment of Britain but was often very naïve. It is one thing to quote politicians on the virtues of the countryside; it is another to expect then to say anything else in rural constituencies. Moreover, if politicians retire to farms, it is not a mark of their lack of interest in production—old men rarely retire to factories. Likewise, legislation regarding 'green belts' is not incompatible with a desire for industrial growth. Konrad Adenauer's Cologne, for example, had designed a green belt years before the British passed their relevant legislation. Yet no one took this to be a sign of anti-industrialism in the Rhineland. Perhaps Wiener was at his most naïve in thinking that landed values necessarily clashed with industrial ones or that the British aristocracy disliked making money. All economic historical research proves him wrong. Frederick of Prussia once described Francis of Lorraine, husband of the Empress Maria Theresa as 'the greatest factory owner of his age'. British and European economic industrial history is one long catalogue of aristocratic landowners who saw coal seams and iron ore beds as part of the produce of their estates, while transport improvements, canals, docks, harbours and railways all required land as much as capital so that for landowners, coal, iron, slate, gravel, clay and even railway lines constituted 'beautiful crops to grow.' Great aristocrats—the Duke of Bridgewater, the Duke of Devonshire, the Duke of Northumberland, the Marquess of Bute, to name just a few—became great developers. Moreover, Wiener's thesis of gentrification may well be a myth. According to recent research considerably less than 10% of all Britain's greater landowners in 1883 were the products of business and professional wealth created after 1780. The Wiener thesis therefore has very little to recommend it; however, among the chattering classes its grip proved quite tenacious. Britain could be written off as a very peculiar—a failing state whose culture and economy were out of touch with the modern world.

Connected to Wiener's views was the assumption, equally strongly held by the chattering classes, that Britain was not merely anti-industrial in spirit, but also antipathetic to science. This view was given its most prominent expression by C. P. Snow in his 'two cultures' lectures in the 1960s in which he argued that there were two cultures in Britain, the literary and the scientific, and that there was a dangerous gap between them. F.R. Leavis famously damned Snow as an 'ignoramus' but Snow's views have since been scientifically demolished by Edgerton. The truth was that Britain in the twentieth century had been a great scientific power. Since 1901 it had obtained about the same number of Nobel prizes as Germany and about half of those awarded to the USA. All other countries were way behind. It was hardly a case, therefore, of resistance to science. Myths notwithstanding, in the late Victorian and Edwardian years, British higher education saw the rapid expansion of science and technology so that by 1929, 55% of university students, according to Edgerton, were studying science, technology or medicine. By 1968, the figure was 65%. While in 1929 scientists and technologists alone made up 30% of the student body, the figure rose to more than 50% in 1967. The British higher education system on this reckoning was much more geared to science and technology than that of other European countries. In the mid-1950s some 44% of British graduates were scientists and technologists, in Germany the figure was 34%, in France 29% and Italy 26%. Indeed, Britain during the 1950s and 1960s had more scientists and engineers per capita than any other major capitalist country.

One reason why these facts have been ignored, according to Edgerton, is that historians of 'decline' like Correlli Barnett, for example, made so much of the differences before 1914 between German and British education. In their scheme of things, Oxbridge and the British civic universities are compared to German scientific ones. This comparison, however, totally ignores the traditional German universities. The fact is that traditional British universities embraced science to a far greater extent than traditional German ones. Cambridge, for example, had the largest school of engineering in Britain until the 1940s. Edgerton remarks: 'Those who link the classics to British decline should recall that German universities were citadels of the classics before 1945.'

Another vital part of the 'declinist' case was that British scientists and engineers had always failed to take up high positions in industry and government. Yet once again, Edgerton refutes this. According to him almost 20% of the leaders of steel firms in the first half of the twentieth century had technical qualifications, about half of them acquired in Oxbridge. In the early 1950s about 20% of members of boards of directors of engineering firms were scientists or technologists and only about 10% were accountants. There is almost no evidence that scientists and technologists were better represented abroad. At the level of senior civil servants, it seems that in the early 1970s the British were much more likely to have had a scientific or mathematical or technical education (26%) than their counterparts in Italy (10%), or Germany (14%). These figures relate to the two highest administrative grades, the equivalent of British permanent and deputy secretaries.

The British record was also much better than popularly supposed if one looks at its record for inventions. Once again, the declinist myth is that Britain gave way to Germany before 1914 and declined in inventiveness thereafter. The truth is that before 1914 Great Britain patented more products per capita in the USA than did Germany and that between the wars the two countries were about level. In the post-war period Britain took the lead until the late 1950s. Turning to R&D, which before the 1940s accounted for only a small proportion of inventions, Britain was –like America and everyone else—behind Germany in dyestuffs. But the true picture is that in general most countries were behind America. By the 1920s and 1930s the US was way ahead of the field. Yet there is no evidence that in these decades Britain was behind Germany.

After 1945, it is often claimed, British industry's share of R&D very definitely fell behind that of Germany and Japan as British governments channelled funds into defence or prestige projects such as Concorde. Since Germany and Japan concentrated on civil R&D, their economies grew faster. Even this sort of rigged comparison does not work, however, since, in fact until the late 1960s, British firms spent ('with their own money', Edgerton emphasises) 15% of what US firms spent on R&D, with German firms spending 14% and Japanese and French ones spending merely 10%. In proportion to the output of manufacturing industry, Britain was way ahead of Germany and Japan into the early 1970s. In the mid-1960s, remarkably, British industry was spending roughly the same proportion of its output on R&D as was US industry. The trouble was, as the British Ministry of Technology discovered in the 1960s, spending on R&D is neither the only nor the chief determinant of national economic growth.

Still, Britain as the richest country in Europe till the 1960s spent the most on invention, innovation and R&D. Its higher education was peculiarly committed to science and technology and its businesses and government had a very high proportion of scientists and engineers. This, of course, is Edgerton's conclusion. However, he wisely puts it into perspective: 'One should not,' he cautions, 'exaggerate contrasts between Britain and other countries. The point is that Britain was not that radically different from the main European economies in its attitude to science and technology; such differences as there were suggest British advantages. Nor should we overestimate Britain's place in world technology—this has certainly been the American century. But what is certain is that Britain has been neither peculiarly anti-science nor anti-industrial.' Edgerton was rightly worried that false interpretations of Britain's scientific past –seeing failure instead of huge success--, were used to explain so-called 'national decline', when the real historical problem requiring explanation was Britain's enduring world prominence. Such false explanations, he feared would merely divert potential students from embarking on successful scientific careers in the future.

Edgerton assumed therefore that Britain's economy was much like other European economies after 1945 save that it had a better record regarding scientific research and innovation. Yet in a couple of key respects –there is no space to mention others—Britain's economy in the 1960s and 1970s was glaringly different. This is why Europhiles could point to greater economic growth in Europe during these years. Their belief was that all the economies were much the same save that Britain's was less innovative, less scientifically oriented and more class-ridden and old-fashioned. Edgerton proved them wrong but the fact remained that Britain's slower economic growth had to be explained. In the years 1953-1973 the average growth in GDP for France was 5.3%, for West Germany 5.5%, for Austria 5.7% and for the UK only 3%. Nonetheless, in some years Britain did very well. In 1959 growth was over 4% in 1961 almost 6% and in 1973 reached 7.4%. Given historical growth rates, Britain's 3% average was by no means bad.

How then had the disparity with Western Europe come about? To some considerable extent, it could be attributed to factors at work in Germany and elsewhere which did not and could not apply to Britain—the rebuilding of cities destroyed by war, the boost given to trade by the dismantling of internal tariffs within the Common Market and by no means least, the continuing switch from agriculture to industry in continental Europe, a process already completed in Britain more than a century before. Equally, two factors applied to Britain which did not apply to the Continent, especially to West Germany, factors which most certainly impeded her economic growth. These were the role of sterling as a reserve currency, or more particularly the effect on sterling of overseas defence spending and the role of trades unions within the British economy. However, once these problems were solved—and solved by British action alone—Britain quickly resumed the role of a leading economy, overtaking Germany in terms of growth.

Sidney Pollard in a devastating study published in 1982 entitled *The Wasting of the British Economy*, made the essential point that sterling was endangered not by any defect in Britain's capacity to trade –the purely private trading account (visibles and invisibles) was invariably in surplus—but by government spending (mainly on defence) overseas. In short, the British domestic economy was sacrificed to please the international bankers and the military, both of whom showed contempt for industry and production. Others, including Malcolm Chalmers, would later reinforce this case.

In Pollard's view, government spending overseas tipped the current account surpluses into deficit and caused balance of payments crises which were dealt with by deflation. The means involved, however, always included the cutting-back of investment which meant that the economy was unable to respond to the next period of expansion. Bottlenecks would then arise, imports would flood in and soon another balance of payments crisis would arise. Once again, investment would be cut, the economy would once again be unable to respond to the upswing and a vicious circle or downward spiral of decline would begin. And what was declining in particular was Britain's industrial base. This process continued, according to Pollard, from the balance of payments crisis of 1947 right through to 1972 when at last the pound was floated and sterling abandoned its role as a reserve currency.

Pollard's point about overseas defence expenditure had already been made in a book published as far back as 1971 by W. A. P. Manser entitled *Britain in Balance: the Myth of Failure*. Manser gave the figures for Britain's balance of payments from 1958 to 1969 (reproduced below from which he concluded: 'The plain testimony of the figures then, is unequivocal. Britain does not run up a commercial deficit. For the cause of her payments imbalance we need look no further than official activity. If there were no government spending, there would be no deficit and no balance of payments problem.'

Manser's Table

	Private Balance (£ million)	Official Balance (£ million)	Overall Balance (£ million)
1958	+ 558	-410	+148

1959	+367	-479	-112
1960	+76	-533	-457
1961	+605	-541	+64
1962	+625	-611	+14
1963	+548	-619	-35
1964	-78	-666	-744
1965	+425	-677	-252
1966	+706	-754	-48
1967	+332	-793	-461
1968	+387	-785	-398
1969	+1326	-924	+384

Manser also pointed out the implications of these figures for Germany or Japan. Had these countries been spending money on overseas defence commitments on the same scale as Britain, Germany in 1966, instead of having a balance of payments surplus of £92 million would have had a deficit of £598 million. Japan's surplus of £120 million would have become a deficit of £300 million. Even taking 'offset costs' for British troops in Germany into consideration, the deficit would still have been £160 million. France, it is true, also had vast overseas defence commitments, but it should be remembered that in contradistinction to Great Britain, France's defence costs during the war in Vietnam were largely paid by the Americans who later subsidised her defence spending on a massive scale through the US Mutual Defense Assistance Act. Manser denied that the British were inefficient or were in any way guilty of 'pricing themselves out of world markets'. The actual prices of world trade were unknown and could not be known, since no statistical service collated them. Nor did it matter, according to Manser, what the British sold.

The Swiss did well with cuckoo clocks, while Britain led Europe in research into aerospace, electrical goods and computing. All the relevant data did not point to 'an inert or inadaptable economy'. In reviewing Manser's book, A. J. P. Taylor wrote: 'It is political dynamite, making nonsense of this country's economic policies over the last forty years. The pundits greeted it with embarrassed silence.'

In 1985, in a book entitles *Paying for Defence: Military Spending and British Decline,* Malcolm Chalmers took Manser's point a great deal further, citing a 1973 study by Kent W. Rothschild which concluded that 'high military expenditure reduces export availabilities in the machinery and transport equipment sector where chances for export expansion have been above average. This brake on the most expansive sector dampens export growth in general. A slow-down in GNP growth follows from this.' Chalmers concluded that resources for the modernisation of civilian industry had been lost with the result that Britain's share of the world market in manufactured exports had deteriorated from 25.5% in 1950 to 8% by 1983. Chalmers also enlarged on Manser's arguments concerning the balance of payments.

Chalmer's Table on Overseas Spending

	Private Balance (£ million)	Official Balance (£ million)	Military element (£ million)	Overall Balance (£ million)
1970-81	+11169	-22747	-7012	-11578
1958-81	+16710	-30330	-9790	-13620

Chalmers also gave data for the percentage of GDP spent by Britain on defence compared to other countries. For the years 1950, 1955, 1960, 1965, 1970, 1975, 1980 and 1983 respectively, the percentages for Great Britain were 6.6,

8.2, 6.5, 5.9, 4.8, 4.9, 5.1, and 5.6. Those for West Germany were 4.4, 4.1, 4.0, 4.3, 3.3, 3.6, 3.3, and 3.4. For Japan the figures were n/a, 1.8, 1.1, 0.9, 0.8, 1.0, 1.0. 1.0, and 1.0. For France the figures were 5.5, 6.4, 6.5, 5.2, 4.2, 3.8, 4.0, 4.2. Only the USA recorded higher percentages (albeit after 1950).

According to Chalmers , Britain's high military budget undermined civilian research and development. For example, by 1956 40% of all professionally qualified scientists and engineers engaged in research and development were working on defence projects. Secondly, almost 60% of these projects were financed from defence funds and nearly two-thirds of the research done by private industry was on defence contracts. The result was that the mechanical engineering industry, shipbuilding and steel employed scarcely any graduate engineers   before the 1960s None the less, Britain still had to look abroad for nuclear weapons and military aircraft. From Chalmers's figures Britain between 1963 and 1980 spent on average about 30% each year of her research and development budget on defence. The equivalent figure for France was about 20% and for West Germany less than 10%.

Theoretically military research could have produced benefits for civilian use. But in Britain's case this does not seemed to have happened. Subsidies for Rolls Royce and Concorde brought a poor return. Indeed, a 1976 report to the Department of Industry stated that the return on a total investment of £1,500 million (at 1974 prices) invested in the civil aerospace industry since 1945 had amounted to less than £150 million. Reports on nuclear energy and naval construction were also dismal. Even the arms race brought a poor return. It may have brought in £2,400 million a year from abroad, but Italy who spent only 40% as much as Britain on defence earned just as much and the French twice as much. Chalmers concluded therefore that British defence spending, particularly but not only overseas defence spending, had an enormously deleterious effect on the British economy. Only with the run-down of the defence budget would matters change. Yet Britain's victory in the Second World War and her post-war obligations as a world power meant that that could not happen quickly. Of course, in the context of defence commitments, EU membership was completely irrelevant.

For many, however, the role of overseas defence spending was not the main factor in explaining Britain's relative decline in the 1960s and 1970s. The main factor, in their opinion, was the role of Britain's trades unions. In the view of Sir Alexander Cairncross, formerly a key advisor to governments and latterly one of the most distinguished economic historians of post-war Britain, the role of balance of payments crises had been much overrated. France had had such crises constantly in the 1950s and Japan had never enjoyed surpluses on current account until the 1960s. Britain's real problem was (Chalmers had also seen this) the steady decline in her share in world exports of manufactured goods which had accelerated since 1945 despite the expansion of the world economy. This explained the constant calls in the British media for 'export-led growth'. Yet, as Cairncross pointed out, there was no logical reason to suppose that more exports would lead to more growth. The opposite was more likely to be true. (See his chapter in volume two of the Cambridge *Economic History of Britain.*) He was by no means alone in his views. Another economic historian wrote in 1981 that 'anyone with the even the slightest interest in Britain's economy since the Second World War can hardly fail to recognise in this {trade union power]a major if not the single most important factor in industrial performance—or the lack of it.' There was certainly plenty of evidence and much of it was summarised in a 1978 study by Stanislaw Gomulka in a   book of essays edited by W. Beckerman for Oxford University Press entitled *Slow Growth in Britain: Causes and Consequences.* A University of Birmingham's

Department of Engineering Production then carried out a study into the working day of workers in 40 engineering and metal-working firms during the years 1968-72. This plus a series of case studies of 45 firms in the period 1970-1974 showed that on average workers spent 16% of their time 'waiting' to use machines, 48% of their time using them, while for about 50% of working time, these machines lay idle. R. Bacon and W. Eltis in their 1976 book on *Britain's Economic Problem: Too Few Producers* discovered that although machine tools used in British industry were on average no older than in the USA, output per machine too and per man was two to three times greater in the USA. Other comparative studies revealed similar results, while the government's 'Think Tank' report on the British car industry found that British car workers operating the same machines produced only half the output of their West German counterparts. (See C. Bean and N. Crafts review of British growth since 1945 in a 1996 Cambridge University book of essays on *Economic Growth in Europe since 1945*)

While British management could certainly not be exonerated from blame, the research conclusively assigned most of the blame for poor British productivity to the workforce and their trade union representatives. This was not on account of their strike record. Professor Turner of Cambridge demonstrated in 1969 that compared with other countries Britain was not peculiarly 'strike-prone'. Rather, it was a matter of demarcation disputes and restrictive practices: too many unions inside any factory, too many men working on any one job, too many arguments over who did what, too many machines lying idle at night or during part of the working day, too little control of shop stewards by national trade union leaders, and too much political influence on the part of those same leaders who often could not deliver the agreement of their members to nation-wide policies negotiated on their behalf. The result, in Cairncross's words was as follows:

'The evidence suggests that when British management sought to raise productivity by the use of modern methods and equipment they found themselves obliged to accept conditions as to manning, operation or pay that cancelled out much of the advantage of making changes that were not insisted upon by the employees of their competitors abroad. Managements also had to devote much of their time to dealing with labour disputes and to contend with a heavy weight of government regulation that absorbed scarce managerial time and deflected effort from innovating tasks of prior importance to economic growth.'

The reasons behind this situation were well known. Given the rise of unemployment in Britain, which was steady, albeit from a low base after 1945, trade unions never really believed that full employment was possible. Folk memories of the thirties and before also played a part. Innovation was always seen as a threat to jobs and many shop stewards and union leaders, some of them quite unrepresentative of their members, simply had no desire to see the capitalist system work successfully. Managers, for their part, with separate canteens, lavatories and other facilities (not to mention different styles of dress and accent) also failed to inculcate into their workforce any sense of identity and loyalty. All this resulted in poor industrial relations and productivity.

Gomulka, Cairncross and others also added another factor to their explanation of Britain's relative economic decline in the 1960s and 1970s—the lack of a 'growth culture' or what Gomulka called 'an environment favourable to business pursuits'. At various times, he pointed out, both Western Europe and Japan had felt the need to 'catch up' with the United States. This had forged a spirit of innovation which success in achieving growth had sustained. Before the late seventies, however, Britain had never felt the need to catch up, having for so long been the leader in a variety of different ways. She had also been complacent about the achievements of others. Finally, there was also the low prestige of industrial management.

During the 1960s nothing was done to remedy this situation. In 1969 Labour's attempts to do so as summarised in the White paper entitled *In Place of Strife* were stifled by internal party dissent led by the then party treasurer, James Callaghan, who recognised his party's financial dependence on the grade unions. When Edward Heath's attempts at industrial reforms failed and the miners came under the syndicalist leadership of Arthur Scargill, the stage was set for further confrontation with the unions. The subsequent failure of the Wilson and Callaghan governments in the 1970s to tame them—indeed, the surrender to the trade union movement by these governments of their whole political credibility—meant that when the unions went on strike during the 'winter of discontent' of 1978-79,the country demanded that the incoming Thatcher government make union reform a priority. As a result the, after eight trade union reform acts, the unions were tamed. Closed shops were outlawed, as was secondary picketing; union bosses had to be elected by secret ballots; 'cooling-off periods' had to precede strikes; strikes themselves had to be approved by ballots; and unions were generally encouraged to accept on-union deals in factories. Mass unemployment also undermined union membership, with the Tories presiding over two recessions. The result was that strikes fell to a historic low and union membership was reduced to about one third of the workforce. The key moment in the destruction of the political power of the unions came with the year-long miners' strike of 1984-5. By the 1990s the unions appeared to be just another pressure group, no longer the country's masters.

Once again therefore the solution to a major problem causing Britain's temporary relative economic decline was found within the domestic political system. Thatcher's parliamentary majorities—not EU membership—brought about reform.

It now seems clear that the supply-side reforms of the Thatcher era (trade union reforms, lower marginal rates of income tax, lower corporation tax etc.) were instrumental in producing a startling growth in productivity that enabled Britain to reverse its record on productivity and to catch up with the Germans. Professor Patrick Minford, for example, has pointed out with regard to productivity gains since 1938 (after which data became available): 'Here the turn-around in relative performance is even more startling. Between 1938 and 1979 German productivity growth was 3.9% per annum; Britain's was less than 1.8%. Between 1979 and 1990, Germany's was 1.5% per annum while Britain's was 3.1%. In each period growth of one is double the other's but the roles are reversed between periods.' He adds: 'no doubt there is also the mature-economy innovation going on too; we know it is in companies like Unilever, Glaxo, Zeneca and many others. But the largest element in the unusual productivity growth of the UK since 1979 must surely be in catch-up. The combination of rising productivity and the lower hourly labour costs in developed Europe, with the capacity to hire flexibly at much lower rates, acts as a magnet for foreign investment.' (See his article in Paul Gillespie's 1996 collection entitled *Britain's European Question: the Issues for Ireland*.) Professor Nicholas Craft has confirmed Minford's statistics. Whereas in the period 1950-79, Britain lagged behind Europe in terms of growth of real output per head and productivity (% per year), the opposite was true for the decade 1979-89. His figures are:

1979-89	UK	European median
GDP/head	2.1	1.9
Labour productivity	1.7	1.6
TFP in business sector	1.5	1.2

(TFP=total factor productivity growth)

In Craft's words: 'The most impressive changes in productivity performance came in manufacturing industry (where)...labour productivity grew faster than West Germany in 26 out of 30 industrial sectors.' In the period 1979-95 GDP per head in Britain France, Germany, and the USA all grew at much the same rate. (See Crafts' article in the Gillespie collection quoted above)

The changes of the Thatcher years meant that both workers and companies were able to improve their positions. According to OECD figures analysed by professor Walter Eltis, in the years 1979 to 1994, the real take-home pay of British production workers increased by almost 26%, while the real take-home pay of German workers grew by less than 3%, the real take-home pay of French workers by less than 2% while the real take-home pay of US workers fell by 7%. Only Japanese workers achieved an increase in real take-home pay in any way comparable to that in Britain. The net-of-tax pay of British workers increased by 24% relative to French workers between 1979 and 1994, by 23% relative to German workers and by 35% in relation to US workers. In fact, the differential in favour of British workers was actually greater still, according to Eltis since OECD figures relate mainly to unskilled workers. But OECD figures for 1994 actually put private consumption per head at purchasing power parities at more or less the same for Britain, France and Germany.

There were other gains for the British economy according to Eltis. Talk of 'the two sides of industry' soon came to an end. So, too, did private sector strikes.

Tax changes, too, had brought in more revenue. In 1978-79 the most highly paid 1% had contributed 11% of total income tax revenues, while by 1995-6 they contributed 15%. In 1979 they had been paying income tax at the rate of 75% or above (Sean Connery left the country in 1978 complaining that he was 'in the 93% tax bracket', while Labour Chancellor Dennis Healey was boasting he would tax the rich 'until the pips squeaked') while in 1996 they were paying no more than 40% but contributing 4% more of national revenue than before. There was also an extraordinary growth in small businesses and self-employment as a result of lower marginal taxation. This growth in small businesses and self-employment meant that unemployment in the UK would become lower than in the EU. There were other results, too. Soon, British labour relations were better than those of France and Germany, her tax rates were lower, and the UK was attracting 40% of all inward investment to the EU. All of this happened, of course, no thanks to the EU—whose regulations and interference merely represented a burden on British industry—but due to Britain's own domestic politics. The speech delivered at Oxford in mid-October 2015 by the Governor of the Bank of England, the Canadian international banker, Mark Carney, who simply attributed British economic success to the 'openness' of the European Union was woefully misinformed. Germany, after making her own domestic, supply-side reforms to her economy in 2003 resumed her economic growth, although after the introduction of the euro, growth in the Eurozone declined, as did growth in the EU generally (see Introduction). Apart from the recession caused by Britain's forced exit from the ERM in 1992, growth in the UK continued until the 2008-2009 world economic crisis at a respectable 3-4%. Then again, Britain's own policy-decisions, including the nationalization of banks, quantitative easing, not to mention her previous decision not to adopt the euro as her currency, saved the day.

According to David Smith, the economics editor of the *Sunday Times* in his column of 4 October 2015, the latest figures demonstrate that since the first quarter of 2010, Britain, like America, has experienced GDP growth of 11.8%, the G7 average has been 9.1% while the EU's is 5.8%. Today, therefore, Great Britain has twice the growth and half the unemployment of the EU. So why remain part of it? Having sorted out our own economic problems by ourselves by winding down our overseas defence commitments, reforming our economy and –crucially—by refusing to adopt the euro, we are once again primed to continue our successful historical trajectory.

Chapter Three: Britain in Europe

Why did Britain join the EEC/EU in the first place? Most people seem to believe that she was forced to, either because she was some sort of economic basket case that needed EEC membership to rejuvenate her economy, or because after the Second World War geopolitics required that she reposition herself away from empire towards Europe. Neither explanation makes the least sense. In the 1950s and 1960s the West European economy was growing on average by 3.5% and 4.5% respectively. In 1959 when Harold Macmillan won his general election victory, real GDP growth in the British economy, according to the Office of National Statistics, was almost 6%. In 1963, when a bemused General de Gaulle, vetoed our first bid to enter the EEC, it was again almost 6%. In 1973, when we entered the EEC, the British economy grew by a record 7.4%. George Osborne would die to achieve such figures. True, on average the British economy did not grow as fast as the economies of France and West Germany in the 1960s and 1970s, but it was not far behind and was sometimes ahead. It was certainly no basket case. And as noted in the previous chapter, what economic problems it had, it cured itself. The EEC, as was seen at the end of chapter one, had no resources or policies to stimulate economic growth in Western Europe after the war; growth arose from the policies of individual leaders in Germany, France and Britain. EU policies—particularly the introduction of the single currency—if anything, proved detrimental to economic growth. Hence there were no overriding economic reasons for Britain to seek to join the EEC from 1961.

The geopolitical argument does not make sense either. Britain after 1945 was certainly no superpower on the level of the USA or the USSR. Still, her standard of living was miles above that of the Soviet Union and she remained a global power of considerable power and wealth. Why then should she abandon her Commonwealth partners--allies and victors in the recent world war just like herself—to join an association of Belgium, Luxembourg, the Netherlands, Italy, France and West Germany? The first four of these countries carried no weight internationally whatsoever. West Germany was part of a divided and militarily occupied nation that still lacked functioning armed forces (which in any case would be strictly controlled by NATO), was full of former Nazis, and had no global influence. France had just lost one costly colonial war in Vietnam and another in Algeria. She was in such a state of political disarray that the Fourth Republic had collapsed in 1958 and General de Gaulle had had to return by dubious political manoeuvring to save the country from civil war.

To any realist student of geopolitics, these countries surely represented a bunch of losers. So why overturn the foreign policy of centuries in a bid to accompany them along a path to 'ever-closer union'? There had to be another reason. And so there was.

As has been seen in chapter one, the experience of World War One had left politicians and intellectuals inside and outside Europe looking to Western, world or European unity as a means of achieving perpetual peace and harmony. Hitler and the Nazis, like the Kaiser and his generals beforehand, believed that a United States of Europe could provide a secure, continental base for a German *Weltherrschaft*. A German-dominated European empire could be the centre for world government. The Nazis, in fact, came up with schemes for a European Economic Community, a European Single Currency and even a European Exchange rate mechanism. European social and other policies were also sketched out. Nor were these policies unpopular during World War Two when Nazi propaganda persuaded millions of Europeans that the Nazi New Order represented Christian civilization. After all, only about 40,000 volunteered to help Republican Spain by joining the International Brigades. Two or three million, on the other hand, volunteered to fight on the Eastern Front against the Bolshevik menace in the name of Christian Europe, this, despite the fact, or perhaps because of it, that the self-styled leader of the new Europe was murdering—or at least taking care of, not everybody knew of the murders—millions of socially and politically undesirable Jews, communists and homosexuals. In 1943, for example, François Mitterrand—later not just the protector of key French fascist war criminals but also the French signatory of the Maastricht Treaty—called upon his fellow Frenchmen to form a militia of 300,000 to be sent to the Eastern Front to defend European civilization from the Soviets. If, after the war, European Union once again became fashionable, there must have been millions of good Europeans who thought their support of the brutal wartime version should be regarded as more premature than criminal.

Ironically, it was not just the Hitlers and the Mosleys of the world who favoured of European Union. The Bolsheviks—Lenin, Trotsky and Stalin—had also given it their blessing. For them, nationalism had been a reactionary, bourgeois phenomenon and by the iron laws of Marxist history had to make way for proletarian internationalism. In the first instance, this would necessitate European Unity, since peoples elsewhere in the world, operating the benighted Asian mode of production, would need to enter a bourgeois phase before Communism could be attempted. On a less theoretical level, Communist Russia was in a good position to take over the rest of Europe anyway.

As history would have it, however, it was to be the proponents of another variety of European integration, who were to take the initiative. These were the European and Anglo-Saxon supporters of liberal internationalism, who appalled by the catastrophe of World War One, misinterpreted history and blamed the world anarchy that followed on the evils of nationalism. Their greatest spokesperson was Woodrow Wilson, and Wilsonian moralists in US administrations were to be among the principal architects of European Union. (To all intents and purposes they included Jean Monnet, who was as much an American diplomat as a French one.) Also included were Europeans and Britons who believed in a new world order based on the legacy of the League of Nations (Monnet had been deputy Secretary-General), some of the British enthusiasts having reached this view via schemes for imperial union. By 1943, not merely Hitler, but Monnet, John Foster Dulles, (who in 1947-48 was Secretary of the American Committee for a United States of Europe), Harold Macmillan and all sorts of people were looking to a United Europe as part of the post-war world. By 1945 western intelligence services (SOE in Britain in particular and the OSS, the forerunner of the CIA in the USA) had become infected with the idea, while in the USA the Council for Foreign relations (a CIA front) saw it as the prime objective of US European policy. Nor, should it be added was this a particularly anti-Soviet policy, since in 1945 there was not much fear of the Soviet Union, still a wartime ally. Indeed, global management—for which European Union was seen as a prerequisite-- would require close cooperation with the Soviets. So, too, would nuclear cooperation and world economic management. Harold Macmillan and others took all this for granted (indeed, this may explain why Macmillan at the end of the war handed over an army of Cossacks to the Soviets to be murdered). Macmillan, indeed, saw the IMF and the World Bank as future instruments of world government. Indeed, a whole generation of leaders who had cooperated against Hitler (condemned as a German nationalist rather than an internationalist; the Soviets could never be tarred with that brush) believed that the real threat after 1945 would still be nationalism not communism. By 1946-47, it is true, with the outbreak of the Cold War it became more difficult for Americans to believe in future cooperation with the Soviets (Macmillan remained much more sanguine—although the true history of his relations with the Soviets remains to be written). On the other hand, the passionate support of leading American statesmen—Stimson, Acheson, McCloy, Harriman, Allen Dulles, John Foster Dulles, David Bruce, George Ball—and newspaper men like Walter Lippmann and James Reston for European Union never wavered. They dined and talked with Monnet in 'total trust' to promote his schemes. Monnet wrote in his *Memoirs* (London, 1978, p. 155): 'The secret elements in these talks, in any case, were less important than the public debate , which helped to move men's minds toward our objective—throwing the weight of American power into the struggle.' In the end that certainly happened. The Schuman Plan, the Pleven Plan and the EEC were as much American as European creations. Bruce himself even drafted clauses of the Schuman Plan. Commentators of all shades agree on this. Professor Gillingham, now at Harvard, wrote in an article in 2007: 'The integration of Europe was, if anything, originally an American project.' Lord Wallace, now Leader of the Liberal Democrats in the House of Lords, but previously an international relations academic specialising in the EU, wrote in another in 1997: 'Western Europe was "America's Europe" '.

For readers unacquainted with the outlook of US statesmen at the end of the Second World War, a good starting point for enlightenment would be to read a wonderful book by America's leading historian of foreign policy, Professor Robert Dallek, entitled *The American Style of Foreign Policy. Culture, Politics and Foreign Affairs.* His chapter on the Second World War, 'World War II: *E Pluribus Unum*', describes with remarkable clarity and wit the American turnabout from isolationism to 'one-worldism'. By 1945, 88% of Americans wanted all the allies in the war to form a post-war force, which 76% of Americans believed should police all countries including America itself. Wendell Wilkie, the Republican presidential opponent of FDR in 1940, sold over a million copies of his book *One World* in 1943, which stated: 'When you fly around the world in forty-nine days, you learn that the world has become small, not only on the map but also in the minds of men. All around the world there are some ideas which millions and millions of men hold in common, almost as if they lived in the same town.' *Life* magazine announced in March 1943 that the Russians were 'one hell of a people...[who] to a remarkable degree...look like Americans, dress like Americans and think like Americans.' The NKVD was 'a national police similar to the FBI'. In April 1944 the *New York Times* declared it no misrepresentation 'to say that Marxist thinking in Soviet Russia is out. The capitalist system, better described as the competitive system, is back.' In the summer of 1943, conservative Congressman John Rankin of Mississippi declared that communism was so unpopular in the Soviet Union that Russians were running it out of the country. Herbert Hoover told the 1944 Republican Convention that Russia was no longer truly communist. FDR said of Stalin 'I would call him something like me...a realist.' Of the Chinese, he said in 1943: '[They] have been, in thought and in objective closer to us Americans than almost any other peoples in the world—the same great ideals. China in the last —less than half a century—has become one of the great democracies of the world.' By 1945 opinion polls demonstrated that it was the firmly held belief of the American people that the peoples of Germany and Japan were also just like them and that only their wartime leaders should be punished.

Given the background sketched out above, it was taken for granted by the US government and US politicians that the European *quid pro quo* for Marshall Aid would be European Union—nothing less than an agreement to create a United States of Europe. Indeed, in order to achieve this they had already created and funded the European Movement—yet another CIA front. (The respected British academic, Professor Richard Aldrich, has published the evidence. See *inter alia* his article on 'OSS, CIA and European Unity: The American Committee on United Europe, 1949-1960', *Diplomacy and Statecraft*, Vol. 8, No.1, March 1997, pp.133-152.) The CIA funnelled at least £380,000 through the American Committee for a United Europe to the European Movement between 1949 and 1955. (See Trevor Barnes, 'The Secret Cold War: The CIA and American foreign policy in Europe, 1946-1956. Part II,' *The Historical Journal*, Vol. 25, No.3, 1982, p. 667.) Winston Churchill lost its leadership when he let the Americans know that he did not favour British membership of a federal Europe, but there were plenty of politicians in Britain and Europe who took CIA funds and Paul-Henri

Spaak, the Belgian prime minister, replaced Churchill as the repository of American hopes. Apart from the naïve idealism of Second World War 'one-worldism', there were several other reasons behind US policy. Clearly it would have been very convenient for America to have just one government in Western Europe to deal with. Again, imitation is the sincerest form of flattery and since American union had worked so well, why should not European Union? Monnet had been FDR's personal emissary to the Free French during the war and had a host of admirers in the State Department, where they were nicknamed 'the theologians'. The issue of Cold War motives is more controversial. The USA certainly hoped that economies of scale produced by European Union would expand the European economy, raise living standards for European workers and help wean them from supporting communist and socialist parties. Stephen E. Ambrose, Eisenhower's distinguished biographer has pointed out that Ike saw no reason why a united Europe should not be given the atom bomb as a Cold War ally and Monnet's own plans for Euratom certainly had the same idea in mind.

Under the Attlee and Churchill governments, however, Britain stood back from these developments. World War II had confirmed her faith in her national institutions, just as defeat and occupation in continental Europe had undermined faith in national institutions there. Britain had been a victor in World War II and had a victor's mentality. Only later would she be infected by the moral defeatism that characterised continental Europe in 1945. Besides, Britain, if not a superpower was still indubitably a world power with a Commonwealth and Empire that straddled the globe and had defence commitments in the Middle and Far East. She could not think of herself as a minor regional actor, for the simple reason that she was not one. Churchill, therefore, took the view that she was 'with Europe but not of it'. And far from isolating herself from Europe at this time, Britain was in the forefront of developments leading to European reconstruction. She may have prevented the European Payments Union from becoming a sort of supranational ministry of economics for Europe under the Marshall Plan and stopped the Council of Europe becoming a directly elected Parliament for Europe, but she began the process of building up European defences against the Soviet threat with the Dunkirk Treaty with France in 1947 and the Brussels Treaty Organisation of 1948. It was British intervention in Greece that saved the Greeks from Stalinism. It was Bevin's diplomacy that helped secure Marshall Aid in 1947 and the establishment of OEEC in the first place, which led in turn to the economic reconstruction of Western Europe. British pressure was also vital in persuading the Americans to establish NATO in 1949. Those who argue that Britain neglected Europe after World War II are either Eurofanatics or are ignorant of British history.

The British, however, were not going to be bounced into American plans for a United States of Europe. If Americans thought of all Europeans as the same, the British were well aware of the differences between them. Besides, it was crazy to expect a people with a parliamentary history going back centuries to amalgamate with nations of little democratic experience, whose most recent acts of statesmanship included the Holocaust, the bombing of British cities, or collaboration with the national enemy. The British were also well aware that ideology was rife in continental Europe after the war and that Communism, Christian Democracy and Socialism, if certainly not replacements for, were the ideological successors of Nazism and Fascism, which themselves might not yet be dead. In every way, therefore, the British people felt—and were absolutely right to feel—closer to their democratic relatives in the English-speaking world, who had taken up arms with them against a united Europe between 1939 and

1945. After all, the democratic credentials of Canadians, Australians, New Zealanders and Americans were not in doubt.

There was, however, a minority of zealots who wanted Britain to merge itself in a United Europe. Most of them were to be found in the Tory and Liberal parties and their most ardent spokesman was Harold Macmillan, who even before the war had supported European federalism. As the process of European integration got under way in the 1950s, he became its main proponent in the British cabinet. His motive was ideological and not the result, as many conventional historians would have it, of some need, as he perceived it, for pragmatic adjustment to events on the continent. Macmillan, like his friend Monnet, whom he had got to know in Algeria during the war, believed in European Union as a preliminary to world government. 'One-worldism' as a means of defeating nationalism was alive and well in both men.

Macmillan, who had advocated a European Coal and Steel Community in a speech in the House of Commons even before the announcement of the Schuman Plan, attempted to nudge British policy under Churchill and Eden in the direction of European federalism. He did not succeed, yet neither did he fail. He arranged for a Treaty of Association to be signed with the ECSC and ensured that a British representative be sent to the Brussels negotiations following the Messina Conference of 1955 on the creation of a European Economic Community. In the late 1950s he pushed the negotiations concerning a European Free Trade Association in the direction of EEC membership and when faced with the prospect of General de Gaulle turning the EEC into a less federalist body, took the risk of submitting a British application for full membership in the hope of using federalist support in the Low Countries and Italy to frustrate the nationalist ambitions of the French president and his new West German ally, Adenauer, who was feared to be a German nationalist.

(Adenauer, like de Gaulle, disliked and distrusted Macmillan.) Monnet met secretly with Macmillan and Heath (his main negotiator) many times in order to facilitate British entry. Indeed, Monnet was informed before the British parliament of the terms of the British application.

This is not the usual view of Macmillan's policy but the archives back it up. Macmillan became prime minister on 10 January 1957 and by 7 November that year, the Under-Secretary of State at the Foreign Office, the Earl of Gosford, was telling the House of Lords that the government was passionately in favour of world disarmament and was 'fully in agreement with world government' which was its ultimate goal and which it would do everything possible to achieve. (*Hansard,* Lords, Vol. 266, pp. 185-194.) The government was also quite aware of the consequences of its policy of joining the EEC. Heath agreed with the view of Lord Kilmuir, the Lord Chancellor and as such the government's chief constitutional advisor, that joining the EEC was not at all like joining NATO insofar as the conferral of a sovereign state's treaty-making powers to an international organisation was 'the first step on the road which leads by way of confederation to the fully federal state.' (National Archives, FO 371/150369, 14 December, 1960.) Both men were European federalists, so agreed to keep this information to themselves. Heath also met with the European Commission President, Professor Walter Hallstein, at the end of 1960 and acknowledged that 'some form of federal Europe' was the ultimate aim of the EEC. (See National Archives, FO 371/ 150369 for Heath's meetings on 16 November and 10 December 1960) In America, the 'theologians' in the State Department were overjoyed at developments, one of them noting: 'with British membership the Common Market could become a true political federation of Europe.' Meanwhile Gladwyn Jebb, acting Secretary-General of the United Nations from October 1945 to February 1946, and British ambassador to Paris from 1954-1960, wrote to Macmillan that once Britain entered the EEC, mere economic considerations would take second place to political integration which would lead to 'an ultimate stage in which it would seem that the UK would not even have the limited autonomy of a Texas.' All this, of course, had to be kept hidden from the public and the House of Commons. (National Archives, PREM, 11/2445, Jebb to Zelueta, Macmillan's private secretary, June, 1961) As Lord Gladwyn, Jebb later became a leading figure in the Liberal Party.

Macmillan's main confident in the civil service was Sir Frank Lee who was brought back from retirement to become joint Permanent Secretary at the Treasury in 1959. He coordinated Macmillan's views with sympathisers in the IMF and World Bank, who, as devotees of Monnet, looked forward to amalgamating the national currencies of Europe and furthering the financial integration of Europe and the USA 'until the West [was] all one country under one government.' (National Archives, PREM 11/3824, 2 February 1961. Directive for Frank Lee's visit to Washington DC) All of this looked forward to and indeed beyond Kennedy's Grand Design for a Transatlantic Free Trade Area in the spirit of US-European 'interdependence'.

Almost immediately after Macmillan's bid to enter the EEC had been announced, Lee was put in charge of a 'Long-Term Policies Committee', which had its first meeting at the end of August 1961. The committee immediately accepted as a long-term goal the replacement of sterling by a European reserve currency, citing support for this in the City. It even questioned whether the UK would exist as an independent sovereign state by the year 2000. (National Archives, CAB 134/1854, 11 August 1961) Macmillan met Monnet in secret on 8 October 1961 and one week later the Long-Term Policies Committee again accepted a European single currency, a European political secretariat, closer integration of national defence forces, the Europeanization of British national education, the creation of a genuine European Parliament and a common European citizenship. (Monnet Papers, Lausanne, Switzerland, Macmillan file, 18 October 1961) It was quite clear, therefore, that whatever Macmillan was telling the British public, Tory MPs, cabinet colleagues or Commonwealth statesmen, in secret, he and Monnet, as soon as the British bid to enter the EEC had been made, were already looking forward to the total absorption of the UK into a federal European state, in which in the words of Gladwyn Jebb, Britain would 'ultimately not even have the limited autonomy of a Texas.' Away from the spotlight, in a speech delivered to MIT in Boston in April 1961, Macmillan laid out his true vision for the world. He declared that it was both necessary and inevitable for international politics to move away from competing nationalisms towards a harmonious and militarily disarmed international order, which would reveal the Cold War struggle to have been nothing more than an irrelevant disagreement as to the best form of social organisation. (Macmillan's relations with the USSR still need to be exposed.) His conclusion was that the world had to prepare for this day by reaching out '...beyond interdependence to consider a greater political union and even union.' It was another plea for One World. (JFK Library, Boston, 3/1/61-5/5/61, folder two, box 170, Macmillan speech to MIT, 7, April 1961)

De Gaulle, of course, in January 1963 vetoed Macmillan's bid to take Great Britain into the EEC. He sensed the American connection, but could not understand the motives behind the bid. Britain already possessed democratic institutions, cheap food, international trading connections, nuclear weapons and global influence. Why bother? But then he was a French patriot, not a proponent of 'one-worldism'.

Macmillan left the torch in the hands of Edward Heath, Douglas Hurd and the other European federalists who by now flourished in the Tory party. In order to consolidate their position, they tightened the alliance with Monnet. This meant joining his Action Committee for a United States of Europe and on 8 December 1968, Monnet wrote to Heath suggesting an annual corporate membership fee for the party of £15,000. The corporate membership would remain secret of course. Lord Plowden could arrange the transfer. (Monnet Papers). Douglas Hurd, Heath's principal private secretary, who met secretly with Monnet in 1968 and 1970 then arranged for this to be done through Lord Edwin Plowden's account in the City. The link to Monnet was obviously considered vital for future prospects of entry into the EEC. Thus Antony Barber, for example, Tory Party Chairman and later Chancellor—and patron of John Major—wrote to Monnet on14 July 1970: '...the role you have played in the making of Europe is legendary; and you will understand why I want as soon as possible to join the distinguished company of those who have enjoyed your friendship and profited from your advice and relied on your unfailing support and enthusiasm for the European cause.' Eventually, of course, Britain was allowed to enter when Georges Pompidou replaced de Gaulle as President of France. There were two reasons for this. First, Pompidou needed a counterweight in Europe to Brandt's resurgent West Germany, whose *Ostpolitik* seemed to threaten to give it the leadership of Europe. Secondly, the British agreed to accept whatever terms were offered, including the surrender of her fishing grounds as part of a new Common Fishing Policy. Con O'Neill, the British civil servant leading negotiations described the bargaining as 'peripheral, accidental and secondary' and in his secret 300-page history of it which lay hidden in the Foreign Office vaults for decades, admitted that his motto had simply been: 'Swallow the lot...And swallow it now.' Hugo Young, the arch-Europhile, *Guardian* columnist, an insider, who was able to read O'Neill's account, commented in his extremely bitter history of Britain's relationship with the EU, *This Blessed Plot*, that the need to descend to this strategy had clearly been Britain's own fault since '*les absents ont toujours tort.*' Clearly, in his view, Britain deserved everything she got for not having been a founder member of the EEC in 1957. Rab Butler, according to Young, commented in 1993: 'I always wonder to what extent Ted [Heath] really understood what it was all about'. Yet, as has been seen, Heath and Macmillan had always been absolutely aware of the final objective of European Union. It was Butler and other cabinet members who had been dupes. Sir Geoffrey Howe, the Solicitor General, also knew the score and completed the betrayal of Parliament's historical supremacy. He simply arranged for the thirteen thousand typed pages of directives and regulations already applying in the EEC plus those that were to follow to be implemented automatically into British law as statutory instruments, to be rubber-stamped by ministers without Parliament having any opportunity to review them. European law became supreme. The glorious history of British parliamentary democracy received a body blow. The legislation was included in a short sub-section of Section Two of the European Communities Bill, which passed by the House of Commons with 309 to 301 votes, with the aid of nine Labour and two Liberal MPs.

Those who took Britain into the EEC never revealed their federalist motives. Their case was always argued on specious economic grounds. 'To trade with Europe', they claimed, 'we have to be part of Europe', which was simply nonsense. Nobody ever claimed that to trade with China, we had to be 'part of China' or to trade with the USA we had to be 'part of the USA' or to trade with Japan we had to be 'part of Japan'. Another Europhile cliché was the supposed need 'to have a seat at the top table' in the EEC in order to trade there;

nobody ever mentioned a need to have such a seat at the top table in China or the USA or other countries in order to trade with them. It was all nonsensical. Countries as diverse as the USA and South Korea do a roaring trade with the EEC without any need to become members or have 'seats at its top table'. Britain was the largest foreign investor in the USA without requiring any political ties or treaties with it and was later the centre of the Eurodollar market without being required to offer any political guarantees. Later still, without itself using the disastrous euro, the City would become the main centre for trade in international financial instruments denominated in euros. Only the *political* objective—'ever closer union', meaning an eventual, federal United States of Europe—required Britain to become a member of the EU as Macmillan, Heath, Hurd, Howe and all the rest knew very well but were determined not to say.

In one twisted sense, however, Macmillan's logic may have had something to it. If it were actually true, 'that to trade with country A' you have to be part of country A', then the world would indeed have required a single government and a single currency. The reason it does not, of course, as any economist will explain, is that currencies have to operate in areas which react to external stimuli in the same way—precisely why the Eurozone is itself not an 'optimal currency area'. The reason why the world does not have a single government is really the same: peoples in different parts of the world have different political histories and traditions, philosophies, standards and expectations. Thus it is no more realistic to expect China and the USA to share a government than to expect Britain and continental Europe to share a currency. To quote Rodney Leach (now Lord Leach), a top City financier, during the debate over Britain entering the euro:

'We have a much lower level of unfunded pensions, something which threatens to double French, German, and Italian national debt by the year 2025; high technology exports are 75% more significant to Britain than they are to Germany; and in general our business is more service and finance oriented; corporate funding in Britain is based on the stock market (on the Continent it is essentially provided by banks); investment overseas plays an exceptionally large role in Britain's economy; by comparison with other major countries we are light on agriculture and long on oil and gas; our system of floating rate finance makes the British house-owner uniquely sensitive to swings in short-term interest rates; and the City has more links with Wall Sreet, Singapore and Hong Kong than with Frankfurt or Paris. Less tangible, after centuries of maritime commerce the British outlook on a number of key issues, from deregulation to free grade, is more Atlanticist than European.'

Clearly Britain did well to retain the pound. There is no pressure at all from other countries to have us reverse that decision. Yet there are still federalists here—Tony Blair, Paddy Ashdown, Richard Branson, Peter Mandelson, Michael Heseltine—who wish to adopt the euro.

The rest of the world would consider it perfectly within our right to leave the European Union as well. US presidential candidates have said they would be willing to make free trade agreements with an independent UK outside the EU, while Gao Jian, Vice-Governor of the China Development Bank, said in April 2013 of a possible British exit: 'It may make a little difference but not much. The City's position as a global financial centre with close connections to Hong Kong would not change. Because of its infrastructure, because of its legal environment, because of its participation in the world, China will definitely use London as a financial hub for many international transactions.' In the same year, Professor Moorad Choudhry, author of *The Principles of Banking*, said: 'The main thing to remember is what attracted firms to London in the first place. Freedom from excessive bureaucracy and high taxation is what led to the Eurobond and FX trading markets siting themselves in London in an earlier era and in this same freedom will ensure that banks and other financial firms stay in the City even after a "Brexit" '. (Both quotes come from Roger Bootle's excellent book of 2014 entitled *THE TROUBLE WITH EUROPE. WHY THE EU ISN'T WORKING. HOW IT CAN BE TRANSFORMED. WHAT COULD TAKE ITS PLACE.*)

The great irony is, however, that despite the federalists' reliance on economic rather than political arguments to advance their case, the EEC has contributed almost nothing to economic growth in Western Europe. As has been noted in previous chapters, economic growth could not be promoted in the first two decades of its existence since its budget was largely devoted to agriculture and fisheries and any marginal growth from tariff cuts could not be easily disentangled from tariff cuts made by EFTA. Growth came instead from the individual policies pursued by a variety of countries usually introduced by supply-side reformers (Erhard, Rueff, Thatcher, Schroeder), policies which were then copied elsewhere. This, as argued in chapter one, had always been the way in which progress had occurred in Europe. The establishment of the EEC, in short, coincided with a period of growth in the world economy, which it did not cause. Likewise, from the 1970s, it coincided with a period of challenges to world economic growth caused by the end of the Bretton Woods System and the oil shocks of 1973 and 1979. During this period it attempted various policies, some to protect failing industries (like the Davignon Plan for steel) and others that experimented with monetary union (the so-called 'Snake', for example). These initiatives, however, largely failed. Then came the resurgence in planning under Delors which led to the launching of the Single Market (only partially completed) and the single currency towards the end of the twentieth century, policies which official EU reports stated would indeed bring increased employment and growth. Unfortunately, as noted in the Introduction, growth in the EU has declined steadily from decade to decade since the 1980s and since the introduction of the euro the economies of Southern Europe have been devastated by large-scale unemployment. Greece, forced to remain inside the Eurozone, has suffered economic and financial catastrophe, while today, in countries as varied as Italy, France, Finland and Portugal, the outlook is decidedly bleak. As Professor Gillingham of Harvard argues in his latest book, *The European Union. An Obituary,* the EEC/EU has had only a marginal influence on European growth for the whole of its history. Again, the need to support the CAP and the Single Market has necessitated a huge volume of bureaucratic red tape to ensure that all the states in the Union adhere to the same regulation. And forcing so many diverse economies together using central legislation has inevitably created opportunities for waste, fraud and market rigidities. These factors have also undermined growth. Indeed, given that the EU has little to do with those aspects of government that impinge most closely on the lives and interests of citizens—education, health, housing, incomes, welfare—and that agriculture, fishing and competitive markets or the lack of them attract scarce attention from most of them, the decline in growth and the economic crisis of the euro has meant that Europhiles cannot really rely on a narrative of economic success—or even relevance—to shore up their federalist ideology.

Despite or because of this, Europhiles have resorted to other arguments since 1973 to maintain support for British membership. A prominent one has been that the European Union has preserved the peace in Europe since the end of the Second World War. Once again, even the slightest review of the evidence refutes the proposition.

The EEC, it should be noted, was formed from 1958. At the height of the Cold War, therefore, it simply did not exist. And the only threat to European peace after 1945 came from the Soviet Union. That threat was met by the establishment of NATO, chiefly by its American, British and Canadian members—whom General de Gaulle denounced as Anglo-Saxons. Certainly, at the height of the Cold War, neither France nor Germany had anything to do with defending the Continent. The French army was fighting a losing war in Vietnam from 1946-1954; between 1954 and 1962 it was fighting another losing war in Algeria. When General de Gaulle returned to power he expelled all NATO forces from France and withdrew France from the military wing of NATO. The Germans were not allowed to have armed forces till 1955, after the collapse of a ludicrous scheme concocted by Monnet for the establishment of a European army. That they were allowed to rearm by the French (who laid down extraordinarily strict conditions—so much for Franco-German cooperation saving the peace!) was due entirely to the fact that the British had agreed to establish the British Army of the Rhine and station 77,000 troops and a tactical air-force in Germany. Even so, the *Bundeswehr* did not become a functioning fighting force till the 1960s. It might also be noticed, that for the entire duration of the Cold War large parts of Western Europe—Sweden, Finland, Ireland, Switzerland, Austria—preferred to remain neutral and that other parts contributed little. The truth, therefore, is quite irrefutable: peace in Europe after 1945 was kept mainly by the Americans, the British and the Canadians.

It is sometimes argued that the European Coal and Steel Community, if of little real economic significance in itself, did help keep the peace by removing from West Germany the means for building up the resources for a renewed war with France. The argument is both anti-German and silly. In the first place, there was no desire on the part of Germans after 1945 to start another war. Their defeat in 1945 had simply been too devastating and overwhelming. In fact, the majority of Germans in the 1950s were opposed to rearmament, which was forced on them by Adenauer and the allies. Their slogan was *ohne mich*, meaning 'without me'. Even had they been foaming at the mouth for revenge, with 500,000 NATO troops stationed in West Germany and another 500,000 Warsaw Pact troops stationed in East Germany, there was nothing they could have done. Thus the ECSC was irrelevant and those who persist in advancing the argument are merely insulting the Germans, who since 1945 have been democratic, law-abiding and pacifist. The German government even lied about its constitution in 1990 to keep its troops out of the first Gulf War. It opposed the second Gulf War and opposed the Anglo-French military attack on Libya to overthrow Gadhafi. It sent a limited number troops to Afghanistan and is not involved in Syria or Iraq. According to the Pew Research Centre, a majority of Germans today would refuse to fight in defence of Poland or the Baltic States if they were attacked by Russia. According to official German government papers leaked to the press, German military hardware is in a deplorable state with submarines, helicopters and tanks unable to function. All of this means that European foreign policy has lacked credibility; indeed, it is wishful thinking to believe in its existence.

The German record also allows one to scoff at the old theme regularly and tediously repeated to British audiences in the past by leading German politicians, that European Unity was necessary to contain a slumbering Teutonic psychopath. Nobody in Britain believed this, yet it was another cliché trotted out by Europhiles to mislead their supposedly benighted British compatriots. More recently, however, as referred to in the introduction, the German treatment of Greece has begun to revive doubts.

A third reason offered in support of European Unity was that it has helped increase democracy. In one sense, but one sense only, there was some truth in this. After ridding themselves of fascist and communist dictatorships (through their own efforts) the newly democratic countries of southern Europe (Spain, Portugal and Greece) and the former Soviet satellite states of Eastern Europe and the Baltic, all entered the European Union in order to consolidate their new democratic institutions. The EU demanded in return that they maintain a free-market economy, a stable democracy, human rights and the rule of law. The former Soviet satellites had also to promise to adopt the euro. On the other hand, it is by no means clear that states like Hungary, Bulgaria and Romania since entering the EU have lived up to the promises they made to secure entry or that the EU has done much to reverse their failings. It also true, that the EU itself during the Euro Crisis replaced the democratically elected prime ministers of Italy and Greece with Brussels-approved technocrats. Since this took place at the same time as the 'Arab Spring', the joke at the time was that whereas the Arabs were seeking to replace unelected old men with democratic leaders, the EU was replacing democratic leaders with unelected old men. Then during the negotiations for the third Greek bailout, Martin Schulz, president of the European Parliament, suggested that the newly elected radical Greek prime minister, Alexis Tsipras should also be replaced by a technocrat. Democracy is not second nature to the EU.

That this should be the case was always self-evident. The right to legislative initiative in the EU has always lain with the Commission and the whole process of thrashing out regulations has been secret, bureaucratic and undemocratic. There is, of course, a European Parliament, but it is a very peculiar body. For a start, unlike even the Zimbabwean Parliament, it has no official opposition. MEPs cannot face their electorates with manifestos that they have any chance of implementing, since the role of the Commission does not change with elections. Elections, therefore, are really meaningless and MEPs remain largely anonymous beings with no accountability to their electorates thanks to the PR

List electoral system that vests power with party bosses. The result is that only 40% of electors bother to vote in European elections and in Britain and France the parties which take the largest share of the votes are those opposed to EU membership (UKIP and the Front National). MEPs in any case seem to have little idea of what is going on and notoriously invented a pseudo-science called 'commitologie' ('committee-ology', based on Sovietology), the science of discovering how the ruling bureaucracy arrives at decisions. Perhaps this is unsurprising. The *Financial Times* in 1992 ran the story that the Commission's new 'openness policy' was being scrapped because it contradicted its 'secrecy rules'. A Principal Administrator of the European Parliament once told the European Research Seminar of the LSE that 'the only people who listen to MEPs are the interpreters.' British contempt for the body was most clearly demonstrated during the Mersey East European Parliamentary by-election of December 1996 when only 11.2% of the electorate bothered to vote. The figure in Liverpool itself was a mere 8.2%. Before recent additional—but still limited-- powers were given to the Parliament by recent EU treaties, the Commission clearly regarded it as a nuisance. To quote that Principal Administrator once again: 'The Council's attitude to Parliament is still one of disdain. Ministers and Commissioners occasionally addressed it, he said, but 'when distilled to their essence you might find a small stain at the bottom of the test tube.' For decades it has been obvious that many MEPs do practically nothing to deserve their salaries (today British UKIP MEPs are the most notorious in this regard according to attendance records). But in 1993, Caroline Jackson, a British Tory MEP, had an official motion accepted by the Chairman of the Parliament, Egon Klepsch, asking how many of her colleagues were still alive. She was particularly worried about a young Neapolitan who had not been seen for ages. According to the report of her speech in the *Swindon*

Evening Advertiser of 17 December 1993, she explained: 'He has not been seen…for more than a year. Is he possibly dead? In which case I am very sorry, but maybe (maybe?) he should not be paid his salary…Some MEPs have not been [here] for years and I wonder how many other dead souls there may be…There are about 100 who never show their faces.' One did turn out to have been shot (A Roman Senator told the LSE European Research Committee that there were 'only' 12 Mafiosi among Italian MEPs) but absenteeism has always had less sinister causes. For example, the Channel Four documentary of 18 October 1996, entitled *Fat Cats*, showed footage of MEPs signing on for their daily allowance of (then) £175 before heading straight for the airport, having done no work at all that day. Despite their journey home by air they were also eligible (without receipts—and until this day they have refused to change this system) for a generous car-mileage allowance, half of which was tax-free. According to the programme an average MEP's allowances and salary made him or her worth £190,000 per year—and that was in 1996.

If MEPs are embarrassing enough, the Commission is a positive danger to parliamentary democracy. Today about one hundred times as many pieces of Brussels regulation are passed by the British parliament as are Acts of parliament in any year. Steve Hilton, until recently David Cameron's chief political advisor, told a seminar at Stanford University in 2014, that forty per cent of the British government's time was spent implementing EU legislation (30 per cent was devoted to British legislation and 30 per cent to unforeseeable political crises). Some government ministries will clearly spend more time than that (DEFRA must spend most of its time on EU regulations). There is no hope, however, of parliament exercising any control of Commission output. When a sub-committee of British MPs, for example, met to debate new metrication directives in 1995 for example, they gave up after fourteen minutes instead of wasting their breath. Opinion polls had demonstrated that 70-90% of the population preferred to retain traditional, imperial weights and measures, but it made no difference. Britain became the only country in the EEC –apart from Eire—to be deprived of the choice of using imperial or metric units. The choice remained legal everywhere else (as it had been in the UK since 1897). EU supporters claim that the Commission is numerically a very small body. Democrats, on the other hand are less concerned about its size than about its power.

The stupidity of Brussels legislation has been demonstrated many times. My own favourite amongst the myriad of weird and wonderful regulations was the one quoted in 1996 in the press claiming that the Commission had decreed that the dung and slurry of all farm animals should henceforth smell the same. (Surely, I thought, this must be apocryphal.) Apparently teams of 'olifactromotists' or sniffers were to be set up to enforce this rule by smelling sachets of air-tight evidence from all over the EU. Whether animals who failed the test were to be dispatched to the abattoir was not revealed. However, the Commission was now open to the charge of being the only executive body in history to decree the harmonization of bullshit--a rather fitting reputation. More tragic was the episode at the end of 1995 when *all* British political parties passed a parliamentary resolution supporting British fishermen against the malpractices of Spanish fishermen. It made no difference. Our European partners supported the Spanish and the minister concerned, William Waldegrave, simply abstained from voting. Perhaps he had drawn the lesson from the 1988 Merchant Shipping Act, which in an attempt to execute the Common Fisheries Policy fairly, outlawed the practice of Spanish ships registering in British ports in order to fish the British fishing quota. This Act was then suspended and subsequently declared illegal by the European Court of Justice. Spanish fishermen who had been fishing the British quota were even granted compensation.

British democracy is undermined in two other ways: first, by the EU's refusal to obey EU law when federalist progress is threatened; secondly, by the evidence that the European political culture is endemically corrupt. It has already been noted in the introduction that the French and Germans were quite happy to breach the terms of the Maastricht Treaty with regard to budget deficits when it suited them, but is the Maastricht Treaty itself legal? British Eurosceptics were quite appalled at the manner in which it was agreed; indeed, the story is highly instructive regarding EU standards.

According to article 236 of the Treaty of Rome, all subsequent European treaties are considered amendments to it and these treaties (amendments) fail if the vote of member states is not unanimous. Yet when the Danes held a referendum on the Maastricht Treaty and voted NO, Europe's leaders went into shock. (So, too, did Danish MEPs who had almost all voted to accept the Treaty.) The Danish Maastricht debate was itself highly instructive. For a start, the fact that a referendum was being held meant that the treaty had to be published. Before then, in the words of the French foreign minister, 'it was meant to be secret.' However, once it had been published in Danish it could be translated into English by Eurosceptics in the UK where the *Sunday Times* published a free version for all its readers. A real debate on the treaty could then start in Great Britain, too, where in the 1992 general election, the major parties had simply ignored the issue. More significantly still, the question arose whether the Treaty would fail. Yet Chancellor Kohl of Germany told the Danes: 'You are just a little people. You cannot dam the Rhine'. They were forced to vote again and pressured into saying YES by a small majority. The cosmetic concessions made to the Danes to bring this about, however, were not written into the Treaty. And had the Danes voted Yes in the first place, there would, of course, have been no chance of opponents of the treaty securing a second vote.

When Ireland voted NO to the Nice Treaty in 2001, she, too, was told to vote again. However, when the French and Dutch voted NO to the very long and quite unreadable Constitutional Treaty of 2005, the outcome of a bizarre, 'consultative' process concocted by and presided over by former French president, Giscard d'Estaing, it was thought that the French were too large a nation to insult by demanding a second vote from them. Instead, Chancellor Angela Merkel of Germany devised the strategy of tweaking the wording of the treaty and calling it something else. In a letter to EU heads of government—it was leaked to the German press—she sought their advice on how 'to use different terminology without changing the legal substance' of the treaty and referred to 'the necessary presentational changes'. Thus another long, almost incomprehensible document was launched known as the Lisbon Treaty and in a speech in London in 2007, former Italian prime minister Giulio Amato explained that EU leaders had deliberately decided that 'the document should be unreadable...Should you succeed in understanding it at first sight there might be some reason for a referendum.' Indeed, even before it was ratified, all the new bodies that depended on it—the European Defence Agency, the External Borders Agency, the Fundamental Rights Agency, the European Public Prosecutor's Office, the new paramilitary structures, etc., etc., were put into place anyway. The real significance of the treaty was to turn the EU from a confederation of independent nation-states into a unitary state with its own legal personality and the right to act as a single state. This crucial constitutional change was now rammed through national parliaments by party whips. But there was no popular mandate for it, the electorates of France and the

Netherlands—both founding members of the EEC having voted NO. There was a strange constitutional hiccup, however, when Ireland found it necessary to hold a referendum after all and again voted NO. Being a 'small country', however, she was told to vote again, just as had happened with the Nice Treaty. The Irish prime minister, Brian Cowan led the new referendum campaign on the slogan, *Yes to Lisbon, Yes to jobs* and won a majority. This happened just before the economy shrank by ten per cent and Brussels thanked him with an austerity package. His party was destroyed in the subsequent general election. The EU attitude to electorates (cf. the Greek Crisis) resembles that of Napoleon, the leader of the pigs in Orwell's *Animal Farm*: 'He would be only too happy to let you make your own decisions for yourselves. But sometimes you might make the wrong decisions, comrades, and then where we would we be?' David Cameron promised a referendum on the Lisbon Treaty to British voters when he was Leader of the Opposition. When he became prime minister in 2010, however, he argued that it was too late to so since Gordon Brown had already signed the treaty. The British people were thus denied the opportunity to express their opinion on this key constitutional development.

The political culture of EU states also seems to be endemically corrupt. One observer writing in the 1990s pointed to various examples. Take Belgium. There a former minister had been charged with the assassination of a former deputy prime minister, while another former deputy prime minister had to endure a parliamentary debate to discover whether his parliamentary immunity would be removed to enable him to face charges if procuring twelve-year-old boys for his sexual gratification. In 1996 the Belgian Secretary General of NATO was forced to resign over corruption charges, after the resignation of the Belgian Foreign Minister on similar grounds. That was after two suicides and one murder. The whole population of the country then took to the streets in protest at the suspected high level of corruption in the judiciary and police force in the aftermath of the country's worst ever paedophile scandal involving the murder of two young girls.

Then there was Italy, where the many-times prime minister, Giulio Andreotti, who signed the Maastricht Treaty, was put on trial three times for being a member of the Mafia who arranged the murder of an Italian journalist who had pointed this out. Witnesses swore to have seen him kissing the *capo di capi* to acknowledge allegiance. It was certainly an open secret that his party's votes in Sicily were arranged by a leading Mafioso. Meanwhile, Andreotti's predecessor as premier, Bettino Craxi languished in permanent exile in Tunisia (until he died) having fled the country facing eight charges of corruption. Before then, he had declared in Parliament that he was indeed corrupt but that so too were all political parties in Italy. No Italian doubted him. A high level of corruption was also evident throughout the civil service. When the house of a top official in the health service was raided, it revealed 250 gold ingots and five Swiss bank accounts. The official concerned claimed only to be saving for his old age. The so-called 'clean hands' revolution of the mid-1990s in Italy, led by local prosecutors, did put an end to the old political party system. However, the main beneficiary of the demise of the Christian Democrats, Communists and other traditional parties turned out to be the media billionaire Silvio Berlusconi, who became Italy's longest-serving prime minister, but who faced constant indictments for income-tax evasion, fraud and other criminal activities. He managed to manipulate the law for some time but was eventually sentenced to community service for procuring the services of under-age prostitutes at his notorious 'bunga-bunga' parties.

The mafia, meanwhile, still collects votes in Sicily for the Italian Right. One of the prime ministers elected in aftermath of the 'clean hands' revolution stated that only a national amnesty would help matters since mafia influence was so widespread. Yet that would simply have freed all jailed Mafiosi to spread their corruption all over again, not merely in Italy but throughout the EU. According to one authority (John Follain, *A Dishonoured Society: The Sicilian Mafia's Threat to Europe*, 1995), the Mafia by the 1990s was defrauding the EU through the CAP of 150-300 billion lire annually. Altogether it was supposed to skim off 3-5% of Italian GDP per annum. Yet Judge Giovanni Falcone, the Mafia's most distinguished victim, warned before he was killed that the Mafia hoped to organise crime not merely on a European scale but globally. Its main advantage was the dismantling of borders in Europe and it welcomed the entry of Eastern European countries into the EU as a means of co-operating with their own huge criminal networks and corrupt politicians. One presumes that Falcone's predictions have by now come true.

Italy and Belgium were hardly alone in their corruption. The *Sunday Times* in the 1990s declared that Spain was even worse. The President of the Bank of Spain had certainly to resign on account of scandal; the Interior minister was accused of running death squads in the Basque Country; while the head of Spanish internal security was prevented from leaving the country with billions of pesetas in a suitcase. In Greece, meanwhile, the 1990s was a period of great amusement. The prime minister, Georges Papandreou, having just escaped a guilty verdict on corruption charges (his co-accused, a more expendable political figure was found guilty but died of a heart attack), proceeded to have his main opponent arrested on similar charges. Greek politics then became even more hilarious when Papandreou divorced his wife and attempted to make his voluptuous mistress, Mimi, the Eva Peron of Greece, an attempt which was only frustrated by his own ill-health and subsequent death, not to mention a stream of pornographic photos of the lady in the Greek press.

France and Germany, unfortunately, behaved scarcely any better. President Giscard d'Estaing of France, for example, the great Europhile behind the Constitutional Convention and subsequent Constitutional Treaty rejected by the French in 2005, had seen his presidency come to a very sour end due to the Bokassa Affair in 1981.This involved accepting bribes from the corrupt dictator of the Central African Republic whom the French had crowned as Emperor there in a mock-Napoleonic ceremony. Emperor Bokassa was later tried for murder and cannibalism by his own people but before then let it be known that he had offered trays full of diamonds as 'presents' to his benefactor Giscard (all of which had been accepted). Giscard claimed to have accepted merely one diamond which he had then sold for charity but he was not widely believed. Perhaps the memory of the de Broglie Affair had had an effect. As a result of this, Giscard's Interior Minister, Prince Poniatowski, had been compelled to resign for having failed to warn an embarrassing political colleague, the Duc de Broglie, who had been involved in gun-running, that a contract had been taken out on his life by a leading French mobster. The Duc, as a result, had been shot down in a Paris street

Under President Mitterrand, Giscard's successor, political life was equally entertaining. The French security services were used to tap the phones of literally thousands of people who might know the secret of the President's officially maintained mistress and daughter. One of those committed suicide in the Elysée Palace. But that was only the tip of the iceberg. One prime minister committed suicide after he was accused of corruption, while a second was committed for trial before the French state on charges of manslaughter. Mitterrand himself was discovered to have aided leading French fascists from the Vichy era and to have presided over all sorts of shady deals. One of his ministers ended up in jail on corruption charges including the rigging of football matches.

If *The Sunday Times* thought Spain a sink of corruption, the *Economist* in its edition of 13-19 July 1996 thought much the same of France. Having reported that the head of French railways had been placed under investigation for the misuse of corporate assets, it commented that he was:

'only the last of an extraordinary long line of luminaries among France's business, financial and political elite to have been caught in a tidal wave of sleaze allegations that have swept across France in the past few years. Hundreds of prominent people have been *mis en examen*. They include eight former government ministers, two former party leaders, dozens of mayors and past and present members of parliament, and one in four of the bosses of France's biggest 40 companies as well as scores of other businessmen. Several have already been convicted. Some like Alain Carignon, former Gaullist communications minister and once mayor of Grenoble, who began serving a four–year sentence a few days ago, have been sent to prison. Some cases have been dropped, but few who have been placed *mis en examen* have emerged unbruised.'

Those convicted included some of France's most prominent politicians such as Bernard Tapie, Henri Emmannuelli and Michel Noir.

Germany, though less prone to corruption scandals than France, Italy Spain, Greece or Belgium, was by no means a stranger to them. In 1996 alone, Dieter Vogel, the chief executive of the German steel and engineering group, Thyssen (with a £17 billion turnover in 1990) was arrested with nine other executives on charges of widespread fraud. Fourteen other executives were also put under investigation. Wolfgang Schaupensteiner, the Frankfurt lawyer then seen as Germany's top anti-corruption prosecutor, was quoted as saying: 'Economic crime has spiralled to levels never seen possible a few years ago. We are witnessing a loss of values in Germany. Moral and ethical principals in

German boardrooms are going to the dogs. Crimes are committed daily and the only thing that seems to matter is profits and selfish materialism.' In the five years between 1987 and 1996, Schaupensteiner initiated proceedings for 1,624 cases of bribery alone and secured more than 300 convictions. In a fraud report compiled by auditors KPMG in 1995, 60% of German managers said they had been victims of white collar crime. Police recorded more than 700,000 cases of fraud and embezzlement in 1996 alone, a rise of 40% since 1993. In one of his largest cases Schaupensteiner investigated more than twenty companies and a group of Frankfurt officials suspected of defrauding Frankfurt airport of millions of D-marks during the building of a new terminal. The case followed the arrest in 1996 of Friedrich Heinemann, former chief executive of the bankrupt Bremer Vulkan shipping group, who was accused of diverting £300 million of government subsidies meant for the modernization of East German shipyards. Investigations were also underway in 1996 into Daimler Benz and Volkswagen.

Nor did German politicians escape charges of corruption. The Flick scandal of the 1980s even involved the Chancellor, Helmut Kohl, although only the Federal Economics Minister Count Lambsdorff and the Speaker of the Federal Parliament, Rainer Barzel, were forced to resign after admitting accepting 0.5 million and 1.7 million D-marks respectively from the Flick Corporation for their political parties. They had done so in return for tax exemptions worth 800 million D-marks. Kohl admitted before a Bundestag investigating committee that as prime minister of Rhineland-Palatinate he had accepted 14,000 D-marks from the company for the local Christian Democrats, but claimed that these contributions had been purely political, i.e. there had been no conditions attached and that he was unaware of any deliberate tax evasion on the part of his local party.

The party funding scandal flared up again in 1999 and thereafter consumed the CDU. Its national treasurer, Walther Leisler Kiep, confessing to taking over 1 million D-Marks in cash from arms dealer Karl Heinz Schreiber. In December 1999 on television Kohl took responsibility for 2 million D-marks of donations accepted illegally during his term in office although he refused to name any donors. This led to him being denounced by Merkel—until then his protégé— and to him being abandoned by the party. Criminal proceedings were instituted against him. He later arranged to give the party 8 million D-marks from other anonymous donors to compensate it for his mismanagement. Meanwhile the scandal led to the resignation of Wolfgang Schäuble as party chairman and the rise of Angela Merkel as party leader.

It would be rather tedious to pursue the annals of European corruption through the Chirac and Sarkozy presidencies in France, or the Rajoy government in Spain with the ruling People's Party there accused of operating an eighteen-year-long slush fund. One could also mention the recent scandals in Germany concerning Volkswagen's emissions' data and the cover-up by German and European transport authorities or even the bribes paid by the German Football Association to FIFA to secure the 2006 world cup. The whole story of Greek corruption unearthed during its recent bailout negotiations could fill a book. Then there are the Berlusconi years in Italy, not to mention the political culture of recent EU member states like Bulgaria, Romania and Hungary. The point is that Britain joined not a new, idealistic experiment in democracy when she entered the EEC but a group of states whose politics were always pretty dodgy—certainly by British standards. Here the scandal of MPs' expenses constitutes by European standards a matter of utter triviality.

Corruption, however, was not something that just happened in individual member states. The EU itself has been notoriously corrupt. This is why for twenty-one years running, up to and including this year, the EU's very own Court of Auditors has refused to approve its accounts. This is a truly astonishing state of affairs but one that the EU now seems to take for granted. What it means is, that were the EU a trading company, it would long ago have been forced to cease trading.

 The annual report by the Court gives chapter and verse on the waste and fraud that has been uncovered in EU accounts. The real trouble is that this amounts, in the words of the auditors themselves, as 'only the tip of the iceberg', to quote John Wiggins, a former British Treasury official who sat on the Court. The sad thing is that whatever the Court recommends to improve matters, nothing is ever done. The 1994 Report, for example, complained: 'Many of the criticisms that have been brought up since 1988 can again be found in the 1993 Report.' Not that the Court has always given the impression of being serious about reforming EU culture. In 1994 it released its report to the press at a party at which journalists were served the best champagne to accompany a lunch of the finest caviar, pâté de fois gras, smoked salmon and asparagus canapés wrapped in gold leaf. The report suggested that the 'tip of the iceberg' amounted to £6 billion or no less than 10% of the EU budget—and all of this was lost in just one year. Such sums at that time could have bought space stations, Channel Tunnels, dozens of hospitals, a few Third World states or most of Europe's political parties. According to the details in the report, a plan to reduce the European wine lake cost £1 billion and increased wine production by 21%; £16 million of grants were awarded to non-existing South African students; £480 million were spent on a palatial debating chamber in Brussels for MEPs despite the fact that they only go there for ten days a year and already have two identical debating chambers in Strasbourg; olive oil producers received £27 million for oil they never bottled; Italian crooks received £8.8 million for airline training courses which never took off; £16 million was paid in holiday expenses to EU officials who stayed at home; Italian beef exporters received £16 million in export subsidies for herding the same cattle back and forth across the same border; while Greek tobacco farmers were paid hundreds of millions of pounds to export unsmokeable tobacco to Albanians who dumped the stuff but who were later paid by the farmers out of their export subsidies. (One official commented: 'It would be cheaper to give the farmers money directly and cut out the tobacco. You could save £300 a year that way.')

Nothing is ever done to stop this rot. For example, when Norman Lamont, as Britain's Chancellor of the Exchequer, put the subject at the top of the agenda for EU finance ministers during the 1992 British presidency of the Council of Ministers, and read out selected sections of the Court's annual report to is colleagues, 'they ostentatiously read their newspapers'. Lamont's successor as Chancellor, the arch-Europhile Kenneth Clarke, reported to the House of Lords' European Communities Committee that several distinguished Greeks had been caught passing off Yugoslav maize as home produce in order to attract EU export subsidies, but had been pardoned by or released from jail by the Papandreou government. In Clarke's own words: 'Some of them have been reinstated quite prominently in public office and one of them I think has now become the head of a state bank.' Yet he concluded: 'I think that we should deplore what the Greeks have done but there is absolutely nothing whatsoever that anybody can do about it.' Shortly afterwards—no doubt on Clarke's advice—Britain voted not to take the Italian government to the European Court to force it to repay billions of pounds of illegal milk subsidies.

One could go on and on. Suffice it to say that on 10 November 2015, the *Times* reported that the Court of Auditors was refusing to approve the EU's accounts for the twenty-first year running. Its failure to sign off spending worth 142.5 billion euros (£101 billion) in 2014, noted the newspaper rather primly, 'will undermine David Cameron's case that the EU can be reformed.' Frustrated auditors called on the Commission to 'analyse the areas of persistently high levels of error as soon as possible.' They again complained that 'weaknesses that we found were very similar to those identified and reported in previous years.'

The Court found that agriculture and rural developing spending worth 57.5 billion euros, the EU's biggest budget heading, continued to be dogged by 'inaccurate or ineligible claims'. In one Spanish case, 'aid was paid for land claimed and recorded as arable land which was in reality a motocross track.' In the Czech Republic, France, Greece, Poland, Slovakia and Spain 'land claimed and paid for as permanent grassland was in reality fully or partly covered with dense shrubs, bushes, trees and rock.' EU regional spending worth 55.7 billion euros, often involving significant construction projects such as road building was marred by 'serious infringement of public procurement rules' aimed at countering corruption. 'Cases of serious failure that we identified in our audit work include unjustified direct award of contracts, unlawful exclusion of bidders as well as cases of conflict of interest and discriminatory selection criteria,' reported the auditors. They also found 'weaknesses' in research budgets overseen by the Commission, including 764,000 euros in costs to a company on a renewable energy research project that was 'almost entirely ineligible'. Nothing much changes, it seems, in the world of EU fraud.

National and EU fraud, not unnaturally, often coincided, sometimes with amazing results. In March 1999, for example, an accusation of fraud made by an obscure accountant led to an announcement by a Committee of Wise Men set up to investigate such allegations that Edith Cresson, the French commissioner, and former French prime minister, had among other offences, awarded a multi-million euro contract for the study of AIDS in Africa to—of all people—her private dentist. Cresson was a notorious figure who had been a disaster as prime minister of France for less than a year. On a visit to Britain she had stated that British men took little interest in her since it was well known that most of them were homosexuals. On the other hand, she was rumoured to have been President Mitterrand's mistress. After her popularity in France fell to a record low of 17%, however, she had been packed off to Brussels, like so many other domestic political failures.

The case against Cresson was devastating. Her accuser, a 'lowly book-keeper' called Paul van Buitenen had attached to his 34 pages of accusation no less than 700 pages of documentation, covering all sorts of instances of fraud in EU foreign aid and tourism programmes as well as hundreds of cases of outright theft in Mme Cresson's directorate. Once he had made his case, the poor man fled to his native Holland after stuffing several more trunk-loads of documents into his car. The Commission President, a Luxembourger called Jacques Santer, did his best to stall but there was little defence against the sheer weight of evidence. The Committee of Wise Men was forced to reveal to the European Parliament 'a catalogue of instances of fraudulently altered tender specifications and disregard for lower tenders., fictitious and double invoicing and inflated fees; unjustified and illegal payments, simple fraud, clear cases of favouritism in employment, and evasion of tax and social security obligations as well as ghost personnel—a low level of overall competence and a pervasive subculture of petty graft, favouritism and criminality.' Clearly Cresson would have to be sacked, but since the European Parliament had no powers to sack an individual commissioner, the whole Commission including Santer himself had to resign. Incredibly, the whistle-blower, van Buitenen, was censured rather than praised before he, too, resigned.

The treatment of van Buitenen set a precedent. When the EU's chief accountant, Marta Andreason, reported that the EU's budget was 'an open till waiting to be robbed', the newly appointed Anti-corruption Commissioner, former British Labour Party leader, Neil Kinnock, fired her. Douglas Watt, another accountant, then posted evidence on his website of high-level corruption in 2003 to discover he, too, was being sacked, even though a secret ballot of his colleagues demonstrated that 40 per cent of them supported his allegations. Yet another Scottish accountant, Robert McCoy, was shunned by his workmates after reporting on the basis of three years' research that most members of the moribund Committee of the Regions charged first-class fares to travel to meetings that they did not attend. He also discovered that half a million dollars' worth of printing contracts had been submitted without tender, only to be rebuked by the president of the Committee concerned for reporting it.

A Danish official,   Dorte Schmidt-Browne was less lucky. She used evidence from a French investigation to report irregularities at Eurostat (the EU's statistical bureau) and 'got smeared by Kinnock and eventually suffered a nervous breakdown', in the words of Professor Gillingham. He added: 'Eurostat was an important agency. EU budget allocations were based on statistics. OLAF (the EU's fraud investigation agency) had invested Eurostat no less than six times, uncovering in the process shell companies, slush funds, and rake-offs. Several dummy companies each received between $3 million and $6 million, which could not be accounted for. Eurostat's director was the principal involved in the machinations, according to the reports. Eurostat also double-charged the Commission and billed for work lifted off the internet. There was, according to a rare parliamentary critic, Jens-Peter Bonde, also a Dane, "...not one crook, two crooks, or five but a parallel system of financing" that continued till July 2003, when the whistle-blowing became ear-splitting.'

Santer's successor as Commission President promised to do better and to clean up the system. In a closed-door session of the Parliament, however, he warned its members that kettles should not call pots black. Kinnock simply called the revelations 'the necessary price of doing business.' Britain had clearly been wise never to have entrusted him with a parliamentary majority. The end result in the words of one expert, Thomas Rupp, endorsed by Gillingham, was 'a kind of fraud which is tolerated because it is within the bounds of what is expected and therefore does not lead to any consequences.'

The British experience of EEC/EU membership was not simply propaganda, dishonesty and fraud; the UK also suffered from the two community policies which took up the lion's share of the budget—namely the Common Agricultural Policy (CAP) and the Common Fisheries Policy (CFP).

The CAP took up 91% of the EEC budget when Britain joined in1973. By the end of the century it was down to about 55%, largely on account of money being spent elsewhere. In actual monetary terms, the agricultural budget had expanded by 973% since 1973. Even John PInder, Chairman of the Federal Trust in London and honorary professor at the College of Europe at Bruges, has had to confess: 'The cost of the CAP remained a heavy burden for the Community with half the budget going to support a sector that employs less than 5 per cent of the working population, much of it for a small minority of the bigger and richer farmers.' (*The European Union. A Very Short Introduction*, p.73.) The policy, of course, originated as a means of bribing the French to enter the EEC in the first place. Thereafter its costs grew exponentially as its generous subsidies to farmers created 'wine lakes' and 'beef' and 'butter mountains'. When the costs at last required a new EU budget settlement, Mrs. Thatcher used the opportunity to force her partners in 1984 at Fontainebleau to 'give her her money back' in the form of a rebate of about two-thirds of the net British contribution. Yet, it was clear that something had to be done to reform the system as a whole. Attempted reforms included the slowing down of expenditure in agriculture to three-quarters of that of the rest of the EU budget after 1988 but after 1992 the Irish commissioner Ray MacSharry secured a cut in the support price of beef of 15 per cent and almost one third in that for cereals. Current levels of farm support remained the same, however, since farmers were compensated with other income guarantees including 'set-aside' payments for leaving cultivated land to lie fallow. This led to the curious situation whereby the Sunday Times could report that Lord Cranborne, then Tory leader in the House of Lords, was receiving £400,000 a year for not planting conifers on his Dorset estates. However, even that distinguished newspaper found it impossible to name Britain's fifteen 'set-aside millionaires'. The Paper did report that among the 53% of British farmers living on incomes less than £20,000 per year, the suicide rate was rising fast. Reform of the CAP came slowly but just over a decade after MacSharry, in 2003, it again moved further away from price-support to income support for farmers. To quote John Pinder once again: 'The new Single Farm Payment (SFP) introduced in 2006 separates (or 'decouples' in the jargon) payment from production: instead farmers are paid to look after their land whether they choose to farm it or not' (author's italics). In other words farmers can now get paid for doing nothing at all to their land. This led George Monbiot, the Guardian columnist to point out in one of his columns that Iain Duncan Smith, notorious for his treatment of welfare recipients, lives on a country estate belonging to his wife that has received more than one million pounds from the CAP under these new arrangements.

It should be pointed out that the CAP has not only been an ecological disaster on a European scale: its effects have been felt world-wide since the agricultural products it exports are dumped on third world countries, thus destroying their hopes for development. Often the EU export subsidies have been larger than the entire GDP of the developing countries that are victimised. Curiously, according to a memorandum from the Ministry of Agriculture, Fisheries and Food of 1995 to the House of Lords European Communities Committee: 'The huge costs of the policy to taxpayers and consumers outweigh any benefit to them...such large transfers into agriculture represent a major misallocation of resources and thus damage the economy as a whole... the policy is extremely complex in detail, hence difficult to administer and giving scope to fraud.' Another section condemned its 'unnecessary trade disputes with third countries', but its most amusing section included a devastating analysis of how several of the CAP's central pillars were unauthorised by the Treaty of Rome. These included the centralised payment of subsidies through Brussels; the intervention system giving producers guaranteed payments; and the erection of tariff barriers against food imported from the outside world. All three main pillars of the CAP were strictly speaking illegal. The document then demonstrated in devastating form how the CAP had failed to honour or be guided by any of the five central objectives laid down in Treaty Article 39. Yet the memorandum concluded that there was no hope of winning support from other EU member states to guide the policy back towards legality. In the words of Dr. Richard North, who analysed the document: 'the British Government makes three simple points: firstly, the CAP is a complete and utter disaster; secondly, its implementation is probably illegal within the context of the Treaty of Rome; and, thirdly, there is no hope whatsoever that anything can be done about it. Apart from that, as they say, there is no problem.' As has been seen, however, there has been some reform. Landowners can now take money from Brussels and do anything they like with it—or not, as the case may be. David Cameron is now pursuing equally meaningful reforms in the EU's political structure.

The other disastrous policy which Britain encountered was the Common Fishing Policy or CFP. It began just hours before the start of negotiations on EEC membership with the Heath government, when the Council of Ministers hastily agreed that such a policy should guarantee 'equal access for all' in Community waters. In this way, all fish were to become a 'common European resource'. Geoffrey Rippon, Heath's main negotiator, meanwhile informed Parliament that the government would resist the CFP. Instead, Heath ordered him to capitulate during the negotiations and simply accept a derogation allowing the UK to retain control over waters out to 12 miles 'until December 31, 1982'. On 13 December 1971 Rippon, none the less, told the House of Commons that Britain had retained full control of her territorial waters and that none of the arrangements made were to be merely transitional. MPs were not given the terms of the concessions made over fishing rights until after the Treaty of Accession had been voted on and signed. It is interesting to note, however, that although Heath managed to persuade the Norwegians to accept similar terms, these contributed significantly to EEC membership being rejected by the people of Norway in a referendum.

After she joined the EEC Britain suffered outrageously from the CFP. The main problems were the system of fish quotas introduced in 1983 and that of decommissioning introduced in 1992, both of which were exacerbated by the size and practices of the Spanish fishing fleet. Eighty per cent of Europe's fish are found in British waters, yet thanks to the quota system, British boats were allowed to catch merely 30-50 per cent of many species. After 1983 the tonnage of fish landed in British ports declined by one third. There were in fact several reasons for this. First, the quota system destroyed fish stocks by forcing fishermen to dump dead fish (of the wrong species) back into the sea. Otherwise they would have been fined for landing them. If too many fish of the right species were caught and put the boat over its quota, they, too, had to be dumped. All this caused great pollution which helped destroy fish stocks. The Spanish, however, paid little attention to any rules. They had very few fish inspectors and they were based in land-locked Madrid. Besides, the huge Spanish fleet (18,000 boats compared to 1,000 British vessels), was known as the 'whore of the sea' and used whatever size of mesh in its nets proved profitable and broke the rules regarding quotas. Worse still, Spanish (and some Dutch boats) developed the practice of registering in British ports to fish the British quota and British legislation to prevent this—as has already been seen—was declared illegal by the European Court of Justice. Soon these 'Anglo-Spanish' and 'Anglo-Dutch' boats were taking a third of the British fish quotas by tonnage (including about half of our plaice and hake quotas) so that some renegade British captains in despair began to sell them their licenses. The situation was made worse since British taxpayers had to pay their share of the EU money used to compensate African states who allowed the Spanish to fish their waters and deplete their stocks. Worst of all, the EU paid subsidies to Spain to modernise and enlarge its fishing fleet.

When quotas became too controversial, a new system was introduced in 1992 of decommissioning boats. The depletion of fishing stocks was used as a reason for this despite the fact that discards continued. Britain's national fleet, in any case, was to be reduced to 209,370 tonnes by the end of 1996 from 250,000 tonnes, which meant that 167 boats would have to be scrapped. In fact some 436 boats were scrapped by 1997 at the cost of £26.2 million. The European Commission in 1997 then demanded a further cut of 40 per cent of the British fishing fleet and proposed changes in mesh sizes and netting use which would advantage the Spanish. British boats began to fly Canadian flags since in 1995 the Canadian government had begun to provide armed protection for Canadian vessels against predatory Spanish vessels off Newfoundland. In the so-called 'tuna war' of the same year in the Bay of Biscay, however, the British government forced British boats to return to port at the behest of the Spanish authorities. Hence EU policy has been to put British waters at the disposal of a mainly Spanish fleet, to pollute the North Sea with discarded fish and to destroy the British fishing fleet and with it Britain's many fishing communities. All of this happened because Edward Heath was determined to take Britain into the EEC at any cost, including a previously unheard of common fishing policy, which our 'partners' deliberately designed to exploit us. The policy of discards was scrapped in 2013 but the dead fish are apparently just sent to landfill. Consumers do not benefit.

Altogether then, Britain's experience of the EEC/EU has been pretty baleful. Both politically and economically there have been almost no benefits.

Chapter Four: The Present Crisis

America's leading historian of the EU, Professor John D. Gillingham III, now at Harvard University's Centre for European Studies, has just completed a book entitled *The European Union. An Obituary.* He has no axe to grind and is remarkably free of that *déformation professionelle* of most US scholars of the EU that equates the nations of Europe with the American colonies of 1776, all destined to achieve a glorious federal union. Today, however, the news from Europe is so monotonously crisis-ridden that Gillingham's views should soon become mainstream. In the first week of December 2015, for example, the Danes voted, against the advice of their government, to shun further cooperation with the EU over matters of home affairs and justice; France's anti-EU National Front party under the leadership of Marine le Pen topped the polls in the first round of the French regional elections; the President of the European Central Bank, 'Super Mario' Draghi was accused of losing his magic touch in economic affairs; a new terrorist incident took place, this time in a London tube station; the President of Estonia in a major speech said: 'Either we do things better or, if we don't, the EU is going to lose its ability as an entity to act in the world.' He was particularly scathing about EU foreign and defence policy. Vladimir Putin had violated every major security treaty from the 1975 Helsinki Final Act to the 1990 Charter of Paris, hence Mr. Ilves continued: 'We have to realise that the post-cold war world era is over. We are in something else now. Peace, love, Woodstock, Kumbaya, let's dramatically slash defence spending and enjoy the peace dividend—that's all over.' (Report in the *Financial Times* of 7 December 2015) The EU, meanwhile, continued to be overwhelmed by an influx of migrants, its economic growth was stalled and there was as yet 'no consensus' over David Cameron's chief demands in his negotiations for a new UK settlement with the EU in the run-up to the Brexit referendum, according to the president of the European Council, Donald Tusk.

The accumulation of bad news, week by week, led even the pro-EU *Guardian* to comment that the Union 'has never looked so temporary and fragile'. Its columnist Ian Traynor on 8 December pointed out that in France, Belgium, Denmark, Sweden, the Netherlands, Austria and Switzerland far-right nationalist parties were leading in the opinion polls while in Hungary and

Poland the nationalist right was already in power. In Britain he added, the Conservative Party, the governing one, also loathed the EU. Meanwhile in the *Financial Times* the day before, Wolfgang Münchau, a regular columnist on Europe, began his piece with the sentence: 'The main characteristic of today's EU is an accumulation of crises.' He added: 'This is no accident. It happens because policies are not working...We have reached this point because the various projects of the union have a negative economic effect on large parts of the European population.' The Danes, he argued were rational to reject closer cooperation with a dysfunctional EU in home affairs and justice in their recent referendum. As for the Italians: 'I would no longer hesitate to say, for example, that the average Italian is worse off because of the euro. The country has had no real growth since it joined the euro, while it had grown at fairly average rates before –and I have heard no rational explanation that does not attribute this to the flaws in European monetary arrangements.' His prediction for the EU was simply informal disintegration. His pessimism was absolutely common. Every other article on the EU by the end of 2015 described it as being in an 'existential crisis'.

Perhaps the crisis will pass. After all, only a decade or so ago commentary of a very different sort was being applauded by the pundits. Both Robert Cooper's book *The Breaking of Nations* and Mark Leonard's *why Europe will run the 21st century* saw the EU as the great hope of the future. Both authors were acolytes of Tony Blair, who himself, of course, had only recently been seen as the great hope for Britain's future. Cooper's book saw the EU as 'post-modern'. He divided the world into 'pre-modern', 'modern' and 'post-modern' states: 'pre-modern' states were those of the third world, 'modern' states those of the third world which had become stable; whereas the EU was the only truly 'post-modern' state. America hovered somewhere between the 'modern' and the 'post-modern'. Cooper dated the emergence of these new entities to the end of the Cold War, an event that changed the nature of the relationship between state and society. The key development was that 'the distinction between domestic and foreign affairs' that characterised the modern period had begun to break down; for European states the erosion of this inside/outside difference meant that they could enjoy life in a quasi-utopian 'post-modern' realm, something akin to Immanuel Kant's vision of a league of states immersed in perpetual peace: 'The postmodern system does not...emphasise sovereignty or the separation of domestic and foreign affairs. The European Union is a highly developed system for mutual interference in each other's domestic affairs, right down to beer and sausages.' Through the pacification of great power and national rivalries, the states of Europe had achieved an evolution in national identity and consciousness, making people less attached to the sovereign nation state.' Indeed the EU regarded international affairs with a new 'moral consciousness'. If all this seemed strange from a Blairite diplomat whose political leader's international humanitarianism had been most famously expressed in 'humanitarian interventions' that led to the bombing of Belgrade and Baghdad, Cooper demonstrated his true colours in his discourse on relations between post- and pre-modern states. This led cynics to suggest that these terms really just meant 'civilised' and 'uncivilised'. Here for example was his advice to post-moderns on how to deal with pre-modern states: 'the post-modern state needs to get used to double standards...when dealing with more old-fashioned kinds of state outside the post-modern limits, Europeans need to revert to the rougher methods of an earlier era—force, pre-emptive attack, deception, whatever is necessary for those who still live...in the jungle.' Perhaps he had already advised his fellow post-modern European, Blair, on Iraq.

Mark Leonard's book marked him out as a modern version of the 'one-worlders' discussed in chapter three of this book. Indeed, he wrote as a sort of reincarnated Monnet or Macmillan. Just like them, he, too, looked forward to a world of regional federations run through the United Nations: '"A Community of Regional Entities" could become the primary co-ordinating body of the United Nations'. It would be better than either the General Assembly or the Security Council for dealing with the two most pressing issues of the day, development and peace-keeping. Nation-states were to be avoided at all costs: 'Instead of hatching deals with China, South Africa, and Brazil, we should aim to make important decisions in EU- Mercosur, ASEM, and EU-AU summits'. In this way, a process would develop which would see 'the emergence of a "New European Century". Not because Europe will run the world as an empire, but because the European way of doing things will have become the world's.' Leonard had little to say about fighting the uncivilised denizens of the third world. He acknowledged the need to use force—Blair was not repudiated--but put the emphasis on other things: 'Europeans have learned the hard way that to promote peace you sometimes need to go to war. But even with the development of European military capabilities, Europeans will rely less on the use of force to shape the world than any other major power. (Note, however, that Europe was still seen as a 'major power' that could 'shape the world'--author.)What makes the European Union unique is that it can bring together its aid, trade and development assistance to prevent hotspots from collapsing into war (Bosnia?, Kosovo? Syria? Libya? Yemen? Ukraine?—author.) Its forces do not just include fighters but an army of 45,000 diplomats, 5,000 police, 2,000 aid-workers for disaster relief, as well as pools of magistrates and election monitors.'

Critics of this kind of fantasy world, needless to say, had an easy time. Philip Cunliffe wrote a review article in *Spiked* on 24 October 2005 and headed it 'ethical imperialism'. The most famous rebuff came with the American scholar Robert Kagan's book *Paradise and Power: America and Europe in the New World Order*. Kagan famously quipped that 'Americans come from Mars and Europeans come from Venus'. His main charge was the obvious one that Europe was simply free-riding on the United States. Her post-modern utopia rested on the fact that her security was provided by NATO which relied overwhelmingly on US fire-power and nuclear weapons. Likewise, when it came to foreign interventions, these always depended on the USA. Libya, of course, would later prove this. Although Britain and France were responsible for starting the intervention, it only proved possible to carry it out due to American willingness to supply missiles and logistics. And for all Leonard's theorising about aid-workers, magistrates, election-monitors, and police preventing hotspots from collapsing into war, the end result was a spectacularly, conflict-ridden, failed state once the Europeans had left.

The obvious defects of European defence and foreign policy were pointed out to his European allies at NATO's Brussels headquarters in a valedictory speech by America's retiring Defense Secretary, Robert Gates, on 10 June 2011:

'...while every alliance member voted for the Libya mission, less than half have participated at all, and fewer than a third have been willing to participate in the strike mission. Frankly, many of those allies sitting on the sidelines do so not because they do not want to participate, but simply because they can't. The military capabilities simply aren't there....

In the past I've worried openly about NATO turning into a two-tiered alliance. Between members who specialise in 'soft' humanitarian, development, peace-keeping and talking tasks, and those conducting the 'hard' combat missions. Between those willing and able to pay the price and bear the burdens of alliance commitments, and those who enjoy the benefits of NATO membership—be they security guarantees or headquarter billets—but don't want to share the risks and the costs. That is no longer a hypothetical worry. We are here today. And it is unacceptable...

Despite the demands of the mission in Afghanistan—the first 'hot' ground war fought in NATO history—total European defense spending declined by one estimate by nearly 15% in the decade following 9/11...Today just five of 28 allies—the USA, UK, France Greece along with Albania—exceed the agreed 2% of GDP spending on defence...

For most of the Cold War US governments could justify defense investments and costly forward bases that made up 50 per cent of all NATO military spending. But some two decades after the collapse of the Berlin Wall, the US share of NATO defense spending has now risen to more than 75 percent—at a time when politically painful budget and benefit cuts are being considered at home.

The blunt reality is that there will be dwindling appetite and patience in the US Congress—and in the American body politic writ large—to expend increasingly precious funds on behalf of nations that are apparently unwilling to devote the necessary resources or make the necessary changes to be serious and capable partners in their own defense. Nations apparently willing and eager for American taxpayers to assume the growing security burden left by reductions to European defense budgets.

Today very little has changed. The British Defence review of 2010 for example reduced British forces to a level not seen since the 1930s and postponed the procurement of vital aircraft and ships, so that Cameron's government only recently proved able to meet the UK's 2% defence spending commitment to NATO by fiddling the books and including items like GCHQ and intelligence in the defence estimates. The Chancellor has now promised much greater investment in defence since the terrorist attacks in Paris in November 2015, but the results will not appear anytime soon. Allusion was made in the introductory chapter to difficulties both the Dutch and German armed forces are having with equipment. Germany, in fact, having been rearmed in the 1950s has been careful not to become involved in war. Excuses were made about her constitution to prevent her participating in the First Gulf War, although her supreme court later ruled that the constitution had provided no obstacle to her taking part. (She was forced to pay a large part of the costs of the war once this was realised.) She opposed the Second Gulf War and did not support the Libyan intervention. She had token forces in Afghanistan and announced the sending of reconnaissance jets and refuelling planes to Syria and a frigate to the Mediterranean to support western action in Syria after the terrorist attack in Paris on 13 November 2015. 1,200 German troops were also to be sent to the Middle East but, they were not to be used in a combat role. In any case, according to Jochen Bittner, a political editor of *Die Zeit,* Merkel sent these troops less for military than for political reasons: 'she is fighting less to destroy Islamic State than to save what is left of European Union solidarity', given the rifts within the EU over the euro, the refugees and tolerance towards Muslims. France and the UK have taken part in air strikes in Iraq and Syria but have only a very limited number of jets each. Both countries still expect to follow the American lead (however feeble), and given their lack of resources, simply have no alternative. NATO is basically still in the situation outlined by Gates in his speech. The legacy of the European Union, particularly of Germany, in world affairs is truly pacifism not peace. Indeed, the late Professor Ulrich Beck in his best-selling book, *German Europe,* described his fellow Germans as 'model pacifists', a description supported by recent data from the Pew Research Centre that found that a majority of Germans today would refuse to fight for the independence of the Baltic States or Poland if they were attacked by Putin's Russia. Bittner, finally, in his article stressed that Merkel had no desire to lose the support of 'Germany's traditionally pacifist mainstream'.

For a period after the end of the Cold War, Europe's military weaknesses did not seem to matter given the naive faith then held in what Francis Fukuyama called 'the end of history' (the much-heralded, ultimate economic and political triumph of the West). It was this that spawned the type of books written by Cooper and Leonard. Yet history had not ended. Events in the Middle East in particular were to demonstrate this, although it was events nearer home that were to challenge the complacency of pacifist Europeans. The speech delivered by the president of Estonia, quoted previously, was an appeal to his fellow Europeans to take the threat of Russia seriously. It had annexed the Crimea, initiated a civil war in Ukraine, and infiltrated troops into Eastern Ukraine to establish de facto breakaway republics there, whose forces, armed with Russian missiles, shot down a civilian Malaysian airliner. Its submarines, aircraft and ships still daily test the defences of NATO allies by entering or approaching their territorial waters and airspace. It is increasing its defence spending to 4% of GDP annually and is rebuilding its conventional and nuclear forces. Its president, Vladimir Putin, openly regrets the downfall of the Soviet Union and apparently wants to re-establish its great power position. He constantly threatens to intervene in the Baltic States and at home has emasculated any opposition, most of whose leaders are imprisoned or assassinated. He is hardly likely to be impressed by post-modern responses from the EU.

For Europe the key figure in negotiations with him has been the German Chancellor, Angela Merkel, who knows Russian from her youth spent in East Germany, where the former KGB spy, Putin, learnt German. In negotiations in Minsk, where the French President François Hollande was also present, an agreement was reached on 11 February 2015, whereby in return for the relinquishing of territory to the rebels and their possession of it legitimised by a generous constitutional settlement inside Ukraine, the Russians and their proxies would cease fighting. There were also provisions for an amnesty and the restoration of food supplies. The situation remains very precarious, however. Fighting has resumed sporadically and at any moment the Russians are well positioned to strike from their positions in Eastern Ukraine south along the Black Sea coast to the Crimea. The *Times* reported on 11 December 2015 that Russia had sent a further 20,000 troops to Ukraine to bolster the rebels, so that there were now 70,000 Russian or rebel forces in the region. President Poroshenko of Ukraine, meanwhile, accused the Russians of intervening in Syria to divert world attention from events in his own country. This may indeed have been one motive behind that intervention, although clearly Russia was determined to prevent the collapse in Syria of the Assad regime. Another likely motive was to demonstrate to NATO the prowess of Russia's new arsenal—hence the deployment of the latest Russian tank there, the T90, the use of its most advanced strategic bomber, the TU160 Blackjack, and the launching of cruise missiles from its Kilo-class submarines. Poroshenko was no doubt correct to see all this as a warning to NATO not to consider intervening in Ukraine. The OSCE, meanwhile, registered a spike in cease-fire violations there causing Ukraine to expect further Russian aggression. NATO is indeed in no position to stop this and unfortunately Ukraine itself is beset by huge external debt problems, dependence on Russian gas, political divisions, widespread corruption, a weak army, and little actual military support from the West, save a few hundred troops sent to train their own ill-equipped forces. Another fascinating but possibly destabilising factor is the political ascent of the former president of Georgia, Mikheil Saakashvili, recently appointed by president Poroshenko of Ukraine as governor of Odessa. Saakashvili has become enormously popular in Ukraine as a successful campaigner against corruption and has been tipped to replace the deeply unpopular prime minister of the country. The trouble is that as president of Georgia he started and lost a war with Russia over South Ossetia in 2008; his new prominence in

Ukraine, therefore, is almost a provocation to Putin, the extent of whose ambition in Ukraine is still unknown. The fact that he agreed to a cease-fire was almost certainly due to Western economic sanctions against Russian firms and individuals. France, under British and US pressure, also refused to deliver two warships it had built for the Russians, while Merkel agreed to sanctions in the face of bitter opposition from German industry, which had heavily invested in Russia. Germany, too, is heavily (40%) dependent on Russian gas supplies. The fact that sanctions were imposed at all was a considerable achievement. So far they have held, but they have to be renewed at given intervals and pressure to relax them from European businessmen suffering from recession should not be underestimated.

Nor should Germany's efforts to appease the Russians. In a letter from the German foreign minister, Frank-Walter Steinmeier to the EU's trade chief, Cecilia Malström, seen by the *Financial Times* and reported there on 2 December 2015, Berlin 'proposed a joint declaration between the EU and Russia offering Moscow the prospect of long-sought investment and energy concessions to create a more integrated economic area from the Atlantic to the Pacific'. Both Angela Merkel and Paul-Claude Juncker backed this bizarre initiative, which, predictably, outraged the East Europeans-- hence the speech from the Estonian president. Meanwhile, the East Europeans are equally incensed by a proposed deal between the Germans and the Russians to build a second gas pipeline from Russia to Germany through the Baltic. Nine EU member states led by Poland are attempting to block it in the European Council. The proposed new Nord Stream 2 pipeline would increase Europe's dependence on the Russian gas monopoly Gazprom. As such the East Europeans argue it contradicts the EU's policy of energy diversification and puts German interests before those of other EU states. It would allow Russia to more easily put political pressure on Eastern European states and blackmail the EU. The USA has also objected that the new pipeline would deprive Ukraine of $2 billion a year in gas transit fees, money either the EU or the IMF would eventually have to make up. Jean-Claude Juncker, however, has refused to consider the matter a political one, declaring that as a purely commercial venture it should be assessed on internal market rules only. The Poles, therefore, do not expect to be successful. Berlin argues that the new pipeline will give Europe added security should Russia cut off gas supplies through Ukraine and that in any case it is simply a private commercial venture. Poland argues that it will cut Ukraine out of the European gas supply chain and will hinder EU plans to integrate energy networks. Nord Stream 1, inaugurated in 2011 was also opposed by Eastern European states that saw it as a means for Russia to control EU gas supplies. Indeed, the then Polish foreign minister, Radoslaw Sikorski, compared it to the Nazi-Soviet Pact of 1939. The pipeline was pushed through none the less with the strong support of the then German Chancellor, Gerhard Schroeder, who signed the deal in his last days in office— before taking up the post of chairman of the Russian company that runs Nord Stream. The dispute over the new pipeline was reported in the *Financial Times* on 30 November 2015. The key point to note, however, is that Germany does not seem to be or feel itself to be in a strong position to resist Russia. Both the dispute over the proposed integrated economic sphere between the EU and the Eurasian Economic Union and that over Nord Stream 2, demonstrate this clearly. Germany realises that an unstable and unreliable Putin could resume his attack on Ukraine any time, hence given her lack of military credibility, her political pacifism, and now her economic appeasement of Russia, all eyes must look to the USA for any credible resistance.

Recently the Americans have indeed promised to budget more resources for Europe. A few new NATO camps have also been established in Eastern Europe and a few US and British troops stationed there as trip-wires. More NATO planes are also patrolling the Baltic skies. The initiative remains with Putin however. He has already grabbed a strategic chunk of territory from a neighbouring sovereign state without resistance and might want to do so again. The EU would simply have to stand by and watch unless NATO offered resistance. It itself could do nothing. But would Germany and other European NATO members endorse military action? Probably not. So much then for Europe running the twenty-first century.

The other strategic problems facing the European Union at present are the control of refugees and terrorism. With regard to the former the civil war in Syria has been the main catalyst forcing literally millions of desperate people to flee for safety to Western Europe. In 2015 probably 1.5 million refugees fled their homes—not only from Syria but from Iraq, Afghanistan, Yemen, Eritrea and several other countries. Being illegal immigrants, they paid 'people-traffickers' to take them on very risky journeys across the Mediterranean, first from Libya to Italy, but later mostly from Turkey to Greece. Both Italy and Greece were soon overwhelmed by the number of migrants—thousands of others, of course, drowned *en voyage*—and simply allowed them to pass through their countries to other member states of the EU, despite the EU's so-called 'Dublin rules' which laid down that all refugees should be registered and processed by the first member state at which they arrived. Hence there was soon a human trail of hundreds of thousands of men, women and children travelling on foot though the Balkans towards their preferred destinations, Germany and Sweden. Amazingly, the EU did nothing at all to provide airlifts for these exhausted people who had literally to walk hundreds if not thousands of miles in appalling conditions to reach their promised lands. It provided no medical services either and often it was left to volunteers along the way to offer succour and sustenance. Later on individual countries provided bus and train services but this was less to help the refugees than to speed them out of individual Balkan countries or Hungary and to ensure they arrived in Austria or Germany. Meanwhile, as the trail grew denser, economic migrants from Albania and Kosovo took the opportunity to swell its ranks. International concern eventually grew and in the summer of 2015 quite unexpectedly Mrs. Merkel let it be known that Germany would welcome all Syrian and other refugees fleeing from war zones, without worrying about the Dublin rules. Her Christian charity was exemplary but her declaration was an open invitation for refugees from all over the world to head for Germany. There was still no airlift, still no network of refugee assembly centres inside or outside the EU from which they could be airlifted; they still had to walk and make it to Germany on their own initiative with the aid of people-traffickers. Mark Leonard's post-modern pools of aid-workers were nowhere to be seen. There were not even official monitors. As the tide of refugees swelled over the million mark towards the end of 2015, there were instead police and soldiers, barbed wire and razor wire fences. Bulgaria built a fence on its border with Turkey, Hungary a fence on its border with Serbia, Slovenia a fence on its border with Croatia, Macedonia a fence along its border with Greece. Austria by the end of the year was erecting a fence 7 foot high and 2.3 miles across along its border with Slovenia. Restricted travel was by now in force at border posts almost everywhere in the EU, partly on account of fears --after the November 13 terror killings in Paris-- that terrorists were travelling among the refugees. Paris took the opportunity not merely to reintroduce border controls but to send more jets to bomb IS in Syria and to introduce new defence spending despite the fact that its budget was already in breach of EU spending rules. Mostly, however, decisions to close borders arose because the national authorities in each country could no longer cope with the numbers arriving. They lacked administrators, procedures, forms and facilities, not to mention accommodation for the refugees themselves. Thus the passport-free Schengen Zone, even in the summer of 2015, seemed doomed to disappear. The German Chancellor, supported by the President of the European Commission suddenly declared, therefore, in August 2015 that all the countries of the Schengen Zone should accept quotas of refugees, admittedly from a total of a mere 160,000, but this provoked outrage among the states of Eastern Europe who took pride in their Christian heritage and had no experience of Muslim citizens. When told they had to comply, they challenged the policy in the European Court. In any case merely 184 refugees agreed to travel to countries outside Germany and Sweden although Austria was expecting nearly 100,000 applications for asylum by the end of the year and by the end of 2015 over a million migrants had reached Germany.

Across Europe meanwhile there had been a backlash against the refugees. Right-wing nationalist parties began to top opinion polls and win election victories in Poland and Austria, while in Germany the PEGIDA movement (Patriotic Europeans Against the Islamisation of the West) held mass rallies against Muslims and the ant-euro, anti-immigrant party, the AFD (*Alternative für Deutschland*) climbed to 10 per cent in opinion polls. In Germany, too, with town and village mayors exhausted attempting to find accommodation and food for thousands and thousands of refugees who sometimes outnumbered the local population, there were 817 'criminal acts' on asylum hostels in 2015—including 68 of arson—as well as a perhaps inevitable political backlash. Horst Seehofer, the head of Merkel's sister party, the Bavarian CSU, demanded an upper limit on refugees—she refused—while an ex-minister wrote a book criticising her mistake in welcoming them in the first place. Her finance minister, Wolfgang Schäuble and home minister, Thomas de Mazière also made it clear that they disagreed with her. As a result, Germany has hinted that refugees from 'safe countries' such as Kosovo, Albania and even Afghanistan will be returned to their homelands. There have also been statements of mixed authority limiting the permitted period of residence of refugees in Germany to two years and forbidding them to bring in family members. All this is in response to the obvious fears of the German public. An opinion poll commissioned for the German news magazine *Der Spiegel* in December 2015 found that 84% believed that the refugee influx would bring 'lasting changes' to the country; 54% foresaw a rising danger from terrorism (the Paris terrorists of November 13 had been able to commute freely between Belgium and France, both states being members of the border-free Schengen Zone, while at least one terrorist had slipped into France from Greece posing as a refugee); 51% percent thought that the crime rate would rise; while 43% foresaw an increase in unemployment.

Clearly, however, there was a need for effective EU action, so that at the very end of 2015 the European Commission promised to announce proposals for a single European Coast and Border Guard to protect its 27,000 -mile sea border as well as a significant expansion of the EU's own responsibilities-- a rather spectacular example, one might think, of closing the stable door long after the horse had bolted. Greece, meanwhile, in an effort to block a threat to be thrown out of the Schengen Area on account of its inefficiency, appealed for more funds and aid from Brussels, thus calling its bluff. Or perhaps not. According to the president of the European Commission the new Coast and Border Guard would have the power to take over control of a country's borders whether the country concerned wanted this or not.(Greece and Italy looked the most likely candidates) The most spectacular development in the saga of the EU's treatment of refugees, however, had already occurred. Merkel decided that the only way to stop the flow was to bribe Turkey and in sheer desperation proved willing to kow-tow to the new strong man of Ankara, Turkey's possibly neo-fascist but certainly megalomaniacal President, Recep Tayyip Erdogan.

After an initial decade as a moderate, reforming and peace-making prime minister, Erdogan had recently turned into a power-driven obsessive, who had built himself a new one-thousand room presidential palace in Ankara, taken over a former Ottoman palace in Istanbul, and had passed a law making those who insulted the president liable to long prison terms. In this way about 350 people had landed up in jail. When he and his close family were investigated for corruption, scores of police and magistrates were either sacked or imprisoned themselves. Determined to make the Turkish presidency an executive rather than a ceremonial post, Erdogan saw his ambition denied in the July 2015 elections by the emergence of the pro-Kurdish HDP (People's Democratic Party) which took 13.1% of the vote, thus denying him a parliamentary majority. Thereafter, he took advantage of IS suicide bombings to resume civil war with Turkey's Kurdish minority and treated opposition with contempt. Refusing to allow a coalition government to emerge, he announced new elections for October and in the run-up to these imprisoned opposition editors, closed down opposition television and radio stations and put several Kurdish towns under martial law. Under these conditions he won a parliamentary majority again but the HDP still managed to clear the 10% barrier to enter parliament and Erdogan, therefore, still lacked the necessary majority to call a referendum on an executive presidency, although he still trying to secure this. After the election, two more opposition editors were arrested and one leading Kurdish human rights' lawyer assassinated.

Merkel herself flew to Ankara on 18 October, before the 1 November election in Turkey giving an election boost to Erdogan, who put on a lavish show of welcome. Agreed in principle was a deal whereby the EU offered Turkey three billion euros annually, visa-free entry for Turkish citizens into the EU and an acceleration of talks on Turkey's full membership of the EU. Amazingly, according to the report in the *Times* on 30 November 2015, part of the bargain included 'taking 400,000 people from Turkish refugee camps every year who will be shared across the EU countries in the Schengen passport-free travel zone'. In return Turkey promised to stem the tide of refugees into Europe and to allow refugees already in Turkey to seek employment and receive education there. There would also be bi-annual talks in future between Turkey and the EU, thus providing summit meetings for Erdogan, who In negotiations apparently showed his contempt for the EU Commission president, telling him that he was a former prime minister of a country (Luxembourg) merely the size of a small Turkish town. Certainly, he struck a hard bargain. He must also have been aware that the chances of Turkey being able to stop all refugees reaching Greece were not high. Publicly, however, he boasted of already doing far more for Syrian refugees than anything Merkel or the EU had done. (Turkey had already accepted two and a half million refugees). More to the point, he had not been questioned about his civil rights record. When asked whether human rights in Turkey had been discussed after EU leaders met to ratify the deal, Merkel replied that they 'did not talk at any great length about that'.

The whole agreement—like Merkel's impulsive decision to allow all refugees from Syria into Germany in the first place--—seems quite bizarre. Only a few years previously Merkel and Schäuble had denounced multiculturalism as a catastrophic failure in Germany, which had proved unable to integrate its Turkish 'guest workers' and their descendants into German society (their rate of unemployment had always remained significantly higher than that of native Germans.) Erdogan himself had worsened relations by visiting Berlin and instructing Turkish families in Germany to put their Turkish heritage and language there first. Now Erdogan and Merkel had agreed to arrangements that outsourced EU border control to Turkey at considerable cost and even looked forward to a future in which 75-80 million Turks could travel around the Schengen Area visa-free with the prospect later of becoming full EU citizens, this despite the previous poor record of German-Turkish relations within the Federal Republic and despite the growing resistance of not merely Eastern Europe to Muslim refugees but the growing fears in the whole of Europe of Islamic terrorism. Nor was it clear, if Turkey sent 400,000 refugees from its camps to the EU every year, yet failed to staunch the influx of new ones from Turkey to Greece as promised, that there would be fewer refugees arriving in the EU in any case.

What was even more bizarre about the agreement was that on 24 November, some days, before its final ratification, Erdogan had ordered his air force to shoot down a Russian military aircraft which had allegedly infringed Turkish airspace. This led to the death of one Russian pilot and subsequently the death of a Russian helicopter pilot on a rescue mission. This was the first time that a NATO country had ever been responsible for downing a Russian aircraft and of course Erdogan demanded—and received—full NATO backing for his actions. He claimed to be outraged at the violation of Turkish sovereignty by the Russian plane, but at the same time rebuffed the objections of the Iraqi government over the regiment of Turkish tanks he had sent into northern Iraq, thus violating its sovereignty. His behaviour seemed unstable. Yet the EU was now dependent on a country whose president had provoked the ire of the equally volatile Vladimir Putin, whose own armed forces were capable at a moment's notice of invading Ukraine—another country regarded by the EU as a future member state.

Worse still, as Germany, France and Britain were showing their determination at long last to challenge IS in Syria, (not that they had any clear or convincing strategy about ending the Syrian civil war) evidence was becoming available that Erdogan, although nominally opposing IS, had been buying oil from it and supporting the so-called Caliphate rather than its enemies in Syria, the Kurds. The latter had been the most efficient military opponents of IS and America's best allied against it, but their ability to deploy in Syria had been severely circumscribed by the Turkish army and their PKK guerrillas had been bombed mercilessly by the Turks. The Russians accused Turkey after it had shot down the Russian plane of colluding with IS in buying its oil and accused Erdogan's own son-in-law of masterminding this operation. The Institute for the Study of Human Rights at Columbia University in New York also built up a long list of evidence of Turkish support of IS. David Graeber, who wrote a full account of Turkey's activities on-line in the *Guardian* on 18 November 2015, called Erdogan 'a man whose tacit political, economic and even military support contributed to Isis's ability to perpetrate the atrocities in Paris, not to mention an endless stream of atrocities inside the Middle East.' Hence the EU is now in bed with a man whose autocratic (neo-fascist) behaviour at home imperils Turkish democracy and domestic tranquillity, a man whose reckless shooting down of a Russian military aircraft has led to vows of revenge from an equally unpredictable Putin, who occupies parts of Ukraine, and a man who has at least tacitly supported NATO's main enemy in the Middle East, Isis, at a time when Angela Merkel is making a military gesture against it to retain some shred of EU solidarity. Moreover, if, as proves likely, the confrontation between Turkey and Russia brings about the cancellation of the proposed gas pipeline between Russia and Turkey, much of Western Europe will remain dependent on the gas pipeline from Russia through Ukraine, which is subject to closure whenever Russia decides to put economic pressure on Ukraine. The EU's dependence on Turkey, therefore, demonstrates that its foreign policy is one of contradictions, desperation and powerlessness; Mrs. Merkel, far from deserving to be Time personality of the Year or a candidate for the Nobel Peace Prize, should be forced to resign. Her leadership of the EU, whether with regard to Greece's bailouts within the Eurozone or in foreign affairs more generally, has been quite lamentable. It makes no sense whatsoever either in terms of post-modern values (*Moralpolitik)* or in terms of old-fashioned reason of state (*Realpolitik*). It is at the heart of the EU's present difficulties.

All this has indeed been Merkel's or Germany's policy. Where the new European External Action Service headed by former Italian foreign minister, Federica Mogherini, fits in it is hard to tell. Her voice has simply been unheard. Yet her new shiny agency which was designed to further 'EU foreign policy' has grown since it was established by the Lisbon Treaty and now has 140 delegations covering 163 countries. It has a staff of 3,474 plus around 3,500 delegated European Commission staff. Its administrative budget comes to £362 million out of the £6.55 billion in the EU's budget for international programmes. Its Brussels headquarters cost £8.5 billion and 29 of its officials earn a basic salary, excluding benefits, of more than the British prime minister. If Britain remains in the EU, the EEAS will eventually replace the Foreign Office in representing British interests abroad and of course will one day provide a permanent EU representative on the UN Security Council replacing those from Britain and France. To be fair, it did have a walk-on role during the negotiations over the Iran nuclear deal, essentially concluded between Iran and the USA, a deal which could yet count as the greatest diplomatic disaster in early twenty-first century history. More recently, the EEAS has been responsible for the growing anti-Israeli policy of the EU. The result is that Israel now holds the EU in contempt and has recently refused to allow any EU diplomats permission to be involved in any Israeli-Palestinian dialogue. Some opinion polls revealed not so long ago that a majority of EU citizens believed that Israel constituted the greatest threat to world peace. One can only hope, given the roles of North Korea, Russia, China, Iran and Isis in world affairs, that EEAS policy does not reflect this view. Finally, EU attempts to spread influence by promoting human rights seem to have got nowhere either. As one of the world's leading contemporary historians, Walter Laqueur, pointed out in his excellent book, *After The Fall. The End of the European Dream and the Decline of a Continent* (New York, 2012), a 2009 EU report on the EU and human rights at the UN read:

'The number of states most fiercely opposed to the EU human rights positions at the UN has swollen to 40 this year from 19 last year. Since the late 1990s when the EU enjoyed the support of over 70% of the General Assembly in human rights votes, support for the EU's human rights position has haemorrhaged: the EU has lost the backing of 13 former allies on human rights votes in the last year—117 of the UN's 192 members now typically vote against the EU.'

So much for Mark Leonard's predictions of the EU running the twenty-first century world by the power of attraction! The truth seems to be that the EU, far from acting like a post-national state with a post-modern morality in international affairs, sees itself simply as another, but bigger nation-state, with a European nationality in the making, and with all the symbols of a nation-stats—passport, flag, anthem, supreme court, parliament, currency, diplomatic, police and intelligence services, coast guard, although still lacking an army. In short, it would like to be a rival to other large nation-states like China, Russia and the USA and like them exert global influence. However, right now it remains an incompetent state entity with no logical or coherent foreign or defence policy to speak of.

Today, therefore, it is mired in crisis over its security, the growing influx of third world refugees and its need to combat Islamic terrorism. Unfortunately, thanks to the desperate decision of Chancellor Merkel to outsource her refugee policy to Turkey, it now has a partner which cannot really be relied upon to stop the flow of refugees in any case yet which can certainly be relied upon to provoke the Russians and double-deal with Isis over the future of the Middle East.

Meanwhile, the euro crisis, which was examined in the introductory chapter of this book, continues. The introduction of the 'single currency' was not of course the first experiment in monetary union and it is instructive to follow the history of previous attempts in relation to the current one as set out by John Mills in an unpublished paper. The so-called 'Snake' which operated between 1966 and 1972, saw the growth rate of all its constituency economies fall between the beginning and the end of its period of operation from 6.9 per cent to -1.2% per cent per annum. This did not, however, stop the drive towards locking the currencies together being resumed after a short interlude following the demise of the 'Snake', during which period the annual growth rate of the European Community, as it was then called, bounced back and achieved an average growth rate of 3.6 per cent per annum. The next attempt to lock exchange rates was the Exchange Rate Mechanism (ERM) which was established in 1979 and in this case the fall in the growth rate from its inception till its collapse in 1993 was from 4.7 per cent per annum to -1.0 per cent. The reason for the decline in performance in both cases was the same:

inflation, particularly for exports, was much lower in Germany than in other constituent economies, nearly all of which as a result tended to run larger and larger deficits in their balance of payments, requiring deflationary measures to keep them under control. This both depressed the growth rates of the weaker Snake and ERM economies and left Germany with increasingly stagnant export markets, so that the German economy's growth rate fell too.

It might therefore have been expected that European leaders would have learned the lesson that locking currencies of highly disparate economies was fraught with problems, but this was not the case. Preparations for the euro went ahead and the long-established currencies of Eurozone members were locked together in 1998 and phased out in 2001.

The performance of the Eurozone, initially, was reasonably if not spectacularly successful. Between 2005 and 2007, the European economies grew by an average of 2 per cent per annum and there was some convergence of GDP per head. The problem was that far too much of the growth depended on low interest rates based on German creditworthiness, which was not matched by that of many other Eurozone members, especially those in the South but also including Ireland. The rapid increases in property prices and building booms which were thus generated were unsustainable, leaving many countries in the Eurozone very poorly positioned to cope with the consequences of the 2008 financial crisis. They were immediately faced with large fiscal and balance of payments deficits to which drastic austerity policies seemed the only answer. The result was that between 2008 and 2013 the Eurozone saw no net growth in GDP at all; meanwhile there was a huge increase in debt, much of it provided in the forms of loans from the European Central Bank to financial institutions in the weaker EU states, which was then channelled into the financing government and national deficits. In 2013 the Spanish government's net operating deficit was 7.5% of GDP while in Greece it was 14.4%. In Italy it was a more modest 3% but Italy had a very high ratio of government debt to GDP at 133% and a worse growth record than any other major Eurozone economy. In 2013, Italian GDP was just under 2% smaller than it had been in 2002.

The Eurozone's 'fundamental problem', according to Mills, is that its constituent economies have levels of competitiveness which are manifestly out of line with one another, especially if the weaker ones were to try to run their affairs with a level of demand which would enable their workforces to operate with a low level of unemployment—say 3 per cent. At the moment, some countries, such as Spain, have managed to achieve a small positive trade balance, but only by implementing austerity policies to hold down imports, which in Spain's case produced an overall unemployment rate of 24% in 2014, with youth unemployment running at more than 50%. As happened with both the Snake and the ERM., the competitiveness of Germany has plunged the other economies of the Eurozone into depression, which in turn has undermined the buoyancy of Germany's export markets.

Things might change if Germany were prepared to implement a large- scale reflationary policy inside Germany and guarantee the debts of other Eurozone states on a mutual basis. However, John Mills concludes: 'But this is highly unlikely, given German memories of the inflation of 1923, because German voters see the other Eurozone countries as the authors of their own misfortunes and see no need to bail them out, and because German academic opinion is much more in thrall to the Austrian School than are Anglo-Saxon economists and has a much greater distrust of the role of the state.'

The countries in Sothern Europe (plus Ireland) which experienced most difficulties were soon known as the PIGS—Portugal, Ireland, Greece and

149

Spain—although Cyprus also required a bailout from the EU. Greece proved the most difficult case as no less than three bailouts were required, the terms of which were dictated by Germany, backed by the EU and the IMF. Notoriously the third bailout negotiations with Greece had to be conducted amid the greatest acrimony with a Greek government led by Alexis Tsipras, whose Syriza Party had just formed a coalition government on a platform of rejecting austerity. Then in the middle of negotiations he held a referendum on whether to accept the terms offered by Berlin and secured a 61% majority for rejection. However, not being willing to abandon the euro, he caved in to the Eurozone's demands and accepted the strict austerity package after all. He then managed to win another election (20 September 2015) to secure a mandate for his surrender and since then, despite two general strikes (supported by the government) and ongoing differences about further cuts to Greek pensions (which have been cut five times already and which face a cut of over yet another billion euros this year out of an overall cut in public spending of 5.7 billion euros in the latest Greek budget), the bailout deal has held. Still, the Greek national debt next year is still expected to reach 186% of GDP and the credibility of its banks—100 billion euros are thought to have left the country during the bailout crisis—is still in doubt. The Greek finance minister, Euclid Tskakalatos, thinks that the dispute over the pension issue could still be a tipping point. In an interview with the *Guardian* on 10 December 2015 he confessed: My biggest worry is...reform fatigue, laws keep coming, laws keep being passed and people don't see the light at the end of the tunnel...It is important that Greeks feel that their sacrifices are paying off.' Hence another euro crisis over Greece could still take place. Meanwhile a left-wing anti-austerity coalition government (including communists) has just taken office in Portugal, although the Portuguese president has demanded that it stick with the euro and with austerity measures agreed with the EU. What will actually happen remains to be determined but developments in Portugal without doubt also leave a question mark over the future of the Eurozone.

More troubling is the fact that it is not only members of the PIGS who are still causing trouble. Even Finland is demonstrating the problems of the 'single currency'. And as Ambrose Evans-Pritchard wrote in a long review of Finnish conditions in the Business Section of the *Daily Telegraph* on 19 November 2015, 'If the euro cannot be made to work for the most competitive country in the EU, who can it work for?' His article began: 'Finland is sliding deeper into economic depression, a prime exhibit of currency failure and an even more unsettling saga for theoretical defenders of the euro than the crucifixion of Greece.' The facts set out in the article were frightening. After six and a half years into the current global expansion, Finland's GDP in 2015 was still six per cent below its previous peak. It was suffering a deeper and more protracted slump than in the recession of the early 1990s or of the Great Depression of the late 1930s. Yet Finland was neither spendthrift nor undisciplined nor technologically backward nor corrupt nor the captive of an entrenched oligarchy—the kind of accusations levelled against the Southern European PIGS. Its public debt of 62 per cent was lower than Germany's and its economy was supposed to be super-flexible. In fact Finland topped the World Economic Forum's Index of Global Competitiveness. It came first in in the entire world for primary schools, higher education and training, innovation, property rights, intellectual property protection, its legal framework, anti-monopoly policies, university R&D links, and the availability of the latest technologies, as well as scientists and engineers. No doubt it was hit by a series of shocks—the collapse of Nokia, the slump in commodity prices, the recession in Russia—but the key fact was that it was trapped by a fixed exchange rate and by the EU's fiscal straightjacket of the Stability Pact. Output shrank a further 0.6 per cent in the third quarter of 2015 threatening to prolong its recession into a fourth year and industrial orders fell 31 per cent in September 2015. Sweden, with a similar economy, however could let its currency take the strain and its GDP is now 8 per cent above its pre-Lehman level.

According to Evans-Pritchard, the divergence between these two economies 'has rekindled Finland's dormant anti-euro movement'. After a petition had collected the necessary 50,000 signatures, the Finnish Parliament was forced to put the possibility of 'Fixit' on its agenda. None the less, Finland's ruling centre-right coalition insisted on pursuing its policy of 'internal devaluation' despite the fact that Finnish household debt was already 120 per cent of GDP. Unsurprisingly perhaps, the Finnish trade unions launched their biggest strikes for two decades in September. During the Greek bailout crisis the Finns had been among the severest critics of the Greeks. Yet to quote Evans-Pritchard once again: 'Its own story was not that different from the EMU disasters that unfolded in the South. Interest rates were too low for Finland's needs during the commodity boom, causing the economy to overheat. Unit labour costs were spiralled up 20pc from 2006 onwards, leaving the country high and dry when the crisis hit after the commodity bubble burst in 2012.' Hence the Eurozone today is under threat not only in the South but in the far North.

Meanwhile the larger member states of the Eurozone are also far from healthy economically. In Italy unemployment figures released in August showed that the number of unemployed Italians between the ages of 15 and 24 jumped from 42.4 per cent to 44.2 per cent, the highest since records began in 1977. As a result overall unemployment rose to 12.7 per cent. In the Eurozone as a whole the percentage of unemployed fell at the same time from 11.6 per cent to 11.1 per cent. In Greece, however, the overall figure was 25.6 per cent and in Spain, 22.5 per cent. Youth unemployment in Greece was 53.2 per cent and in Spain 49.2 per cent. In the Eurozone as a whole it was 22.5 per cent. (See the *Times* for 1 August 2015). Yet it is the French economy that is perhaps the most worrying. It is trapped in an economic slump reminiscent of the inter-war years of 1929-1936 under the Gold Standard. Unemployment in October jumped to 10.8 per cent overall but among young adults aged 18 to 24 it was 24 per cent and among those without qualifications, 46 per cent. According to Professor Jacques Sapir of the EHESS in Paris, quoted in the *Daily Telegraph* on 8 December 2015, French industry was being slowly hollowed out. The dripping effect of closures—typically 150 or 200 workers at a time—was creating areas of 'rural misery' in Burgundy and Lorraine and parts of Normandy and Picardy. Abrose Evans-Pritchard, the author of the article, added: 'Yet monetary union has played its part too. The Eurozone's twin policies of fiscal and monetary contraction from 2011 to 2014 aborted recovery and led to a deep recession that went on long enough to create lasting economic damage through labour "hysteresis"'. France's Leviathan state, he recorded, had now ballooned to 57 per cent of GDP—'a Nordic level without Nordic flexibility'. According to OECD only 25 per cent of those aged 60 to 64 was actually in work due to early retirement. Public pensions, therefore, gobbled up 14 per cent of French GDP.

The chief beneficiary of the French economic malaise has been Marine Le Pen, leader of France's National Front. She boasts that her first order as French President would be to draw up plans for the restoration of the franc. In her words: 'The euro ceases to exist the moment that France leaves. What are they going to do about it, send in the tanks?' The euro-crisis is far from over.

Unfortunately, the foreign policy, refugee and euro crises are not the only problems facing the EU. The sad truth is that it still seems mired in corruption—and at the very top. Both the President of the European Commission, Jean-Paul Juncker, and the President of the Eurogroup, Jeroen Dijsselbloem, have been revealed as complicit in first organising and then covering up the fact that Benelux countries deliberately formulated tax evasion scams with multinational companies whereby for example companies like Amazon and Fiat had their 'corporate taxes pushed down to almost nothing'. Apparently there were hundreds of such deals, but both men made sure that the European Parliament's Special Committee on Tax Rulings as well as committees of the European Council were for years denied the relevant documents to investigate them by the European Commission and the European Council itself and their actions have only become known as a result of the so-called 'Luxleaks' scandal. The documents have now been seen and analysed in a long article on *Spiegel Online* on 11 June 2015 by Marcus Becker, Peter Müller and Christoph Pauly, yet shamefully, the story has never been taken up by the British media.

Juncker had the gall to boast to the G20 summit in Ankara in Antalya in Turkey this year that the EU was demonstrating leadership in the field of 'harmful tax competition' and that other countries should follow its example. Yet this was the very man who has prime minister of Luxembourg had turned it into a tax haven. The scam centred on so-called 'hybrid tax instruments' and 'patent boxes' which were used as means to allow companies to transfer their tax liabilities to Benelux countries where they paid practically no tax. After the 'patent' box scheme was introduced in Belgium in 2007, corporation tax there fell from 33.99% to 6.80%; in Luxembourg it fell from29.22% to 5.84%. Under the scheme larger subsidiaries of these companies in higher-tax countries would transfer their profits to the subsidiaries in Benelux ones. The governments of the Benelux countries were thus able to collect billions, but not merely were other EU countries disadvantaged but small and medium sized companies were exclude from the scheme. All the other member states, according to *Spiegel Online* knew exactly what was going on. The German member of the Working Group on Tax Questions, for example, filed a cable to Berlin in March 2013 noting that there had been repeated doubts 'about the harmlessness' of various tax models 'mostly having to do with the license box rules of LUX and NDL'. Yet nothing could be done since the Benelux countries warded off all proposed changes by regularly co-ordinating decisions before group meetings. The Benelux countries also refused to reveal any information about their tax rulings for four full years before the Luxleaks scandal broke. The authors of the article revealing everything state: 'The documents seen by SPIEGEL reveal that what EU agencies have long been denying, is in fact mass-scale cheating with the help of the tax law. Internal EU documents show how companies took advantage of patent boxes to simply sign their licenses, copyrights, patents or marketing rights over to their subsidiaries in Luxembourg or The Hague, allowing them to cash in on sweetheart deals in those countries. It didn't matter whether the research had actually taken place in these countries, either.' So far nothing has happened. Luxembourg and the Netherlands are stalling even compromise proposals for reform and Juncker himself, although prime minister of Luxembourg for eighteen years denies playing any part in establishing these tax schemes. The European Parliament even agreed to go lightly on him in its investigations, given the protection he has received from the President of the European Parliament, Martin Schulz and the leader of the Conservative European People's Party there, Manfred Weber. Yet according to SPIEGEL, 'the former head of tax issues at Amazon testified last December that Juncker, in personal meetings between the two, had offered to assist the on-line retailer in setting up a tax home in Luxembourg. He said that the Luxembourg government had behaved as a "business partner"'. So much for Juncker, the model European, President of the European Commission, who turns out to be someone who has regularly cheated on his EU partners. The same duplicity can be levied at the former finance minister If the Netherlands, now President of the Euro-group, Jeroen Dijsselbloem. If it is true that a fish rots from the head, this obviously is a saying that applies to the European Union.

Its example, moreover, is being followed by European banks. The *Financial Times* reported on30 November 2015 that Deutsche Bank has also 'been devising complex international tax avoidance strategies for its largest corporate clients, even as G20 governments and the OECD attempt to close loopholes involving moving money to other jurisdictions.' Yet in a recent statement, OECD said governments were losing $240 billion in revenue because of corporate tax avoidance.

In the case of Deutsche bank, the financial instruments involved were profit participating instruments or PPI. Under the proposed strategy a Deutsche Bank client in Brazil would have co-invested with the bank's Austria unit in a newly established Austrian entity. The Austrian entity would then take the funds and lend them back to the corporate client in a jurisdiction outside of Brazil with favourable withholding tax rules, such as another European country such as Luxembourg. Both the client and Deutsche Bank would benefit from the 'profits' of the Austrian entity—generated from the loan terms—and pay them as dividends that would also qualify for tax exemptions. The whole scheme would be covered up as an exercise in raising finance or some other disguise. Once the scheme was leaked, Deutsche Bank declared that although it was not illegal, it had not proceeded with it: 'These transactions were never executed', said the bank in a statement. No doubt, given the scrupulousness with which the EU monitors tax evasion, many other schemes are operating very profitably.

Today, therefore, the European Union faces a crisis of credibility not merely regarding its ability to protect the security and currency of its citizens but even regarding its probity.

Chapter Five: Brexit

Given the seriousness of the crisis in which the EU now finds itself, it is difficult to believe that it will survive in the long term or even in the medium term. In Britain, as everywhere else in Europe, Eurosceptic opinion is growing all the time and there is no chance that David Cameron will be able to manipulate the media or the public in the way that Harold Wilson managed to do in 1975 to secure a majority for remaining in the EU in his referendum of that year. Wilson's government concentrated, it is true, on grossly exaggerating purely cosmetic changes to our terms of membership, much as Cameron's is doing today. But then the media and big business were totally on board. Today that is not the case. Headlines such as *City lines up to buy ticket out of Europe* and *City grandees throw weight behind Brexit* (both from the *Sunday Times*) are becoming more common as are quotes from leading businessmen such as Jim Ratcliffe—'the billionaire boss of Britain's largest private company'—who said: 'I think the UK would be perfectly successful as a standalone country, part of the European marketplace like Norway and Switzerland but without the expensive EU bureaucracy.' Ratcliffe added: 'The Brits are perfectly capable of managing the Brits and don't need Brussels telling them how to manage things. I just don't believe in the concept of a United States of Europe. It's not viable and it's not a concept anyone really wants.' In his view, 'Brits are British,

Italians are Italians and Germans are German. Look at America. Californians, Texans, they see themselves as Americans, so do New Yorkers, but it's not that way in Europe and never will be. We are independent countries.' (*The Times*, 20/7/2015) The *Guardian* on 18 May 2015 had a headline that ran: 'EU exit may be in UK interest, says top firm,' and quoted JCB chief executive Graeme Macdonald as saying: 'I think it would be better because I don't think it would make a blind bit of difference to trade with Europe. There has been far too much scaremongering about things like jobs. I don't think we or Brussels will put up trade barriers.' Lord Bamford, the JCB chairman, told the BBC that the UK 'could negotiate as our own country rather than being one of 28 nations'. Other leading figures such as those behind the headlines already quoted from the *Sunday Times* could be cited *ad nauseam*. The fact to note, though, is the confidence behind such voices these days. The EU seems so bureaucratic, undemocratic and thoroughly *passé* to them, that any idea that they have somehow lost touch with the *Zeitgeist* seems quite bizarre. This was certainly not the case in 1975, when Eurosceptics were accused of having been left behind by the locomotive of European progress.

Today, it is the Europhiles who are clearly on the defensive—and little wonder given the record of the EU that has been set out in previous chapters. Take for example the words of Lord Rose of Monewden, head of the 'Remain' or 'In' campaign. He says that should the UK leave the EU it will be hard to tell if it has made any difference. To quote him in full: 'Nothing is going to happen if we come out of Europe in the first five years, probably. There will be absolutely no change. Then, if you look back ten years later, there will have been some change, and if you look back 15 years later, there will have been some. It's not until you get to twenty years later that there's probably going to be some movement...It's not going to be a step change or somebody's going to turn the lights out and we're all suddenly going to find that we can't go to France, it's going to be a gentle process.' (*The Times,* 17/10/2015.) The lack of dynamism is astonishing. Of course, there is a good chance that, while Lord Rose is waiting for the gentle process of reaction to set in over two decades, the EU will have ceased to exist once other member states have followed Britain's example. The defensiveness seen in Lord Rose's interview is not the only indication of lack of confidence in the 'Remain' camp. Perhaps the knowledge that most of those involved in it have previously campaigned for British membership of the ERM and the adoption of the euro as Britain's currency has also taken the wind out of its sails. This certainly restricts the number of business 'experts' it can produce and undermines the credibility of the usual Europhile spokespersons like Lord Mandelson, Sir Martin Sorrell and Sir Richard Branson. But even the support it is getting from the EU itself is proving bizarre. Take the following report which appeared in *The Daily Telegraph* on 24 October 2015 under the headline 'Farmers forced to erect EU billboards if they have grant':

'Farmers will be forced to erect billboards publicising the fact that they have received EU grants, or face having the money clawed back.

Thousands of landowners have been told they must put up permanent billboards which can be seen by the public, or face financial penalties.

The new regulations led to warnings that farmers were being forced to become part of the "EU propaganda machine" in the run-up to a referendum on Britain's membership.

Eurosceptic MPs are concerned that the EU will use its financial clout and funding for British institutions to try to Influence the result of the vote.

There is also concern that the billboards could blight rural areas and popular walks, as up to 11,000 landowners could take part in the scheme. Landowners receiving at least £38,825 of EU funding must erect a plaque of at least one square foot, while those getting 7,765 must display an A3 poster.'

With friends like that, who needs enemies? Meanwhile, a red-faced Bank of England has accidentally released its plan for a secret task force known as Project Bookend to prepare for a possible Brexit, this despite a House of

Commons committee being told by the Chancellor of the Exchequer that the government and civil service are making no contingency plans whatsoever—a singular example of hubris perhaps.

It would seem then that during the forthcoming referendum, the positive side of the campaign will come from the 'Leave' camp and the negative side from the 'Remain' camp. Spokespersons for the latter will surely not all be as mealy-mouthed as their leader Lord Rose. On the other hand they will have little positive news to relay from today's EU. Scare tactics, therefore, will be the order of the day for them.

There will also be another fundamental difference between the two sides. The Leave campaign will be adamant that the EU is at heart a political project aimed at establishing a federal Europe, as indeed its own literature, quoted in the introductory chapter of this book, makes abundantly clear. The 'Remain' campaign will seek to avoid political and constitutional issues altogether. This has always been its strategy and it will again concentrate on economic matters. Yet, as this book has emphasised, to trade with China, you don't have to be part of China. To trade with the EU, as the Europhiles themselves insist, you do need to be part of the EU, accepting EU citizenship, passports, institutions, courts, laws, policies, parliament, flag, anthem, diplomatic service and all the rest. The referendum debate, therefore, will certainly not just be about commercial regulations. The price of access to the Single Market, silently but wholeheartedly endorsed by the Europhiles themselves, is the political and constitutional superstructure described above. The cost of the Single Market should be measured, therefore, not in monetary values but in Britain's lack of freedom and independence.

Europhile scare-mongering and myth-making will take a variety of forms. Foreign manufacturers will continue to be primed, as they already have been, to state that leaving the EU would cause them to reconsider remaining in the UK. Just days before Cameron promised a referendum, for example, Kenneth Gregor, Jaguar Land Rover's chief financial officer, warned that leaving the EU would create 'barriers' and jeopardise a 'relatively stable relationship' with Britain. Honda, Hyundai and BMW all said similar things as did the Japanese government. Yet, Jonathan Lindsell, EU Research Fellow at the respected think-tank *Civitas* pointed out in an article in the *Times* dated 21 April 2015, entitled 'Alarm over EU exit should be taken with a pinch of salt', that despite Cameron's promise of an EU referendum and despite gains for UKIP, foreign companies had subsequently invested more than £2.7 billion in British automobile manufacturing. Ford, for example, whose chief executive Stephen Odell, warned that Brexit would be 'devastating for the British economy', confirmed a £24 million high-tech investment in Brigend in Wales just months after the prime minister's speech. Likewise the American (GM) –owned Bentley, announced an £800 million investment in Crewe. After UKIP won the Euro-elections in May 2014, Vauxhall created 550 new jobs in Cheshire and Luton (although Vauxhall's chairman later stated that in his view Brexit would not make any difference to UK trade), while Jaguar Land Rover, owned by Tata Motors, announced 250 new jobs as part of a £200 million new investment. Along with a £1.5 billion pledge to its Solihull plant, this was especially odd, given the above-quoted remarks of its chief financial officer. It would seem, therefore, some nervous statements notwithstanding, foreign investors would continue to invest in Britain after Brexit—just as they did after Britain rejected the euro or after it left the ERM.

The fear over job losses if Britain were to leave the EU is one which the Remain Campaign—particularly Liberal Democrats like Nick Clegg—emphasises by repeating that three million would be at stake. This derives from a deliberate misinterpretation of research published in 2000 by the National Institute of Economic and Social Research (NIESR). Its annual report merely stated that up to 3.2 million jobs were 'associated directly with' the export of goods and services to the EU. The then director of NIESR, Martin Weale, denounced the Europhile spin as 'pure Goebbels'. Indeed, the same paragraph of the report stated:

'In conjunction with the potential gains of withdrawing from the Common Agricultural Policy and no longer paying net fiscal contributions to the EU, there is a case that withdrawal from the EU might actually offer net economic benefits.'

The Europhiles also claim that withdrawal would lead to a major tariff war between the UK and the EU, an assertion which once again is pure scare-mongering. After all, 6.5 million jobs in the EU are directly associated with the export of goods and services to the UK. The EU sells far more to us than we do to it. So why would political leaders on both sides of the Channel risk ten million jobs in total on a tariff war? What would be the point? The global average tariff is less than 3 per cent according to most recent World Bank data. In Europe and the United States the respective figures are 1.04 per cent and 1.46 per cent. Switzerland charges zero and Norway 1.09 per cent. The rules of the World Trade Organisation (WTO) moreover follow the principle of 'the most favoured nation' which means that member states cannot impose arbitrarily high tariffs on one another. Hence a trade war would be illegal. Even if one occurred against WTO rules, who could possibly benefit?

The UK, as has been seen, would be in a more advantageous situation than the EU. But why bother? Most probably a free trade treaty would be signed abolishing tariffs altogether. Nor is there any need to examine present arrangements between the EU and Norway and Switzerland. The British economy is so much bigger and trade with the EU so much greater that any deal would most likely be unique.

Despite all that, it is only fair to concede that the figures just employed are all averages and apply to a Britain still within the EU. Clearly if the UK were to leave the EU, the figures would be different and vary for different industries. Detailed research by Business for Britain has found that outside the EU the average tariff on British goods would be 4.4%, for those exported to the EU, 4.3%. Yet the key fact to bear in mind is that the extra costs on British exporters would be far lower than the amount Britain would gain by no longer being an EU member state. In simple terms, using the data for 2013, Britain would pay, in a worst case scenario under WTO rules, just 66p in tariffs for every £1 gained by no longer paying membership dues. In fact, 0.43% of GDP as a maximum trade cost for being outside the EU would be an extremely manageable amount. In 2013 from a gross transfer of £19.4 billion in funds to the EU, Britain paid net costs of £11.3 billion. Given that the cost of tariffs borne by industry under the worst case scenario under WTO rules would be £7.4 billion, it would appear that Britain two years ago paid a premium of almost £4 billion just to trade within the EU. That was the equivalent of £145.36 per household or £82.58 for every individual in the country. Since then, these costs have risen. The overall costs of Britain's EU membership have been estimated in the past at 4% of her annual GDP by both the Cardiff Business School and the respected think-tank *Ciivitas*. The latter even suggested that if 'opportunity costs' were factored in the figure would rise to 10% of GDP annually. That would be over £100 billion per annum. Business for Britain has calculated the annual saving per household of Brexit at £933, made up from £145 from the savings from the EU budget contribution, £361 from savings from the CAP, £186 from savings from the CFP, £70 from landfill tax imposed on councils through the EU, £20 from EU burdens passed on through council tax, £5 from product shelf prices and £146 from cheaper clothing.

Returning to the issue of possible tariffs on British industries in the aftermath of Brexit and attempting to be absolutely fair, Business for Britain conceded in a worst case scenario, that some industries—41 in particular—would be disproportionately affected by British withdrawal. The worst cases were beef and dairy farming, beer and whisky exporters, clothing and footwear sellers, and motor cars. Altogether these industries would bear £5.4 billion of the £7.4 billion costs. Yet any post-Brexit British government would be in a strong position to target compensatory measures towards these industries from the £11.3 billion (more today) saved *annually* by leaving the EU. In any case, the exports of these industries amount to less than half of one per cent of British GDP. Brexit, in short, hardly looks likely to start a tariff war or disadvantage British exporters. There would be so much money saved from our annual EU membership fee that any industries disproportionately affected could expect to be well compensated. (The 1,500- page report on Brexit, entitled *Change or Go* was published by Business for Britain last year.) However, most would benefit. For example, the 90 per cent of British companies which today do no trade with the EU but are forced to implement EU standards and regulations would all be free of them.

Another industry which would benefit from leaving the EU is financial services, concentrated in the square mile of the City of London. In 2012 the City's contribution to UK national income was 3.7%. It is home to 15,000 companies and is expected to generate £61 billion of income a year by 2025 and to employ 435,700 people. London is the world's premier global financial centre followed by New York, Hong Kong and Singapore. European financial centres such as Frankfurt, Paris and Amsterdam have never been able to compete with it, although Luxembourg, according to a report in the *Daily Telegraph* of 4 December 2015, 'will attempt to challenge London to become Europe's leading financial centre in the next five years with a new plan to attract businesses from global banking to financial technology startups.' European jealousy of London certainly increased with the creation of the Eurozone, with Christian Noyer, Governor of the Bank of France, for example, saying in December 2012: 'We are not against some business being done in London but the bulk of euro-business should be under our control. That is the consequence of the choice by the UK to remain outside the euro area.' And indeed, the European Central Bank was only stopped from preventing the City dealing in euro-denominated financial instruments, when this was decreed illegal by the European Court of Justice. That decision, however, could still be appealed. When a European Banking Authority was agreed in 2012 in the wake of the great financial crisis, George Osborne, the British Chancellor of the Exchequer, persuaded EU member states to agree to a so-called 'double majority lock', whereby all laws passing through that institution had to go through two rounds of voting: first by Eurozone states and then by non-Eurozone states. Majorities in both rounds are required for legislation to pass. This allows a majority of non-Eurozone states effectively to veto laws that are not in their interest. Yet it has subsequently emerged that were the number of non-Eurozone states to fall to four or fewer in coming years, the lock would cease to exist and the City would be at the mercy of Eurozone law-makers and financiers.

This is no idle threat. EU regulation is a huge worry for the City. Most commentators list bankers' caps and bonuses, the transaction tax, the Basel III rules and opposition to over-the-counter derivatives as their main anxieties. If only it were that simple. For example on 16 October 2011, the business editor of the *Sunday Telegraph*, Kamal Ahmed, stated in his column: 'There are at present at least 38 pieces of European regulation that have either been passed or are being formulated in Brussels that will have an impact on the financial services sector. That, at least, is according to a detailed chart by the regulation experts from Clifford Chance...Some senior figures in the Treasury think the final number could be even higher and top 50.' His column lists all of Clifford Chance's thirty eight -from Over- the –Counter Derivatives Regulation to the Financial Transaction Tax. It would take too long to cover all the regulations involved but the AIFM or Alternative Fund Managers Directive that was published in the EU's *Official Journal* on 1 July 2011 and came into force on 21 July 2011 can be taken as an example. Originally targeted at 'risky' hedge-funds it has ended up hitting investment trusts and unit trusts with an extra layer of bureaucracy. According to a study conducted by Deloitte most UK-based asset managers believe that the AIFM Directive could reduce the competitiveness of the EU's alternative investment funds industry because of the compliance the regulations impose on it. These managers-- from hedge funds, private equity and real estate sectors-- also believe that the directive will reduce the number of non-EU managers operating within the EU. Another example is the Solvency II regulations for the insurance industry. The *Sunday Telegraph* on 4 March 2012 reported that EU regulations would 'harm' UK insurers in an article that began: 'European politicians are plotting regulatory reforms that will penalise UK insurance companies and cut retirement incomes by up to 20pc, senior industry sources have warned.' Prudential is quoted as stating that it is considering moving to Hong Kong to avoid the full impact of the regulations. The Association of British Insurers is quoted fearing that the new rules will prevent them from competing globally. Complaints about regulations of course are not restricted to the City. Quite recently the *Guardian* reported (28 July 2105) that 'The Scottish government is turning to increased private sector funding to pay for a multibillion-pound spending programme for dozens of new hospitals, schools, roads and community centres as a result of a Brussels ruling that has delayed large public spending projects in Scotland'. However, the City is of prime importance. And in the words of Peter Cruddas, founder of CMC Markets, in an article in the *Daily Telegraph* on 24 June 2015: 'Independent polling...reveals that those working in the City, and not just at the top of it, believe the cost of regulation from the EU outweighs the gains. Given that only 34% of the UK's earnings from financial services exports came from the EU in 2013 and the proportion of financial assets accounted for by the top five EU economies is projected to fall from 27% to 12.5 % by 2050, patience with the cost of regulation for a declining market is surely declining itself.' Inside the EU, however, it is very difficult for the UK o protect the City of London. As has been seen, the 'double majority lock' of non-Eurozone member states inside the European Bankers' Authority is likely to disappear. The UK, moreover, has only 9.5 per cent of the seats in the European Parliament and only 17 per cent of the votes in the Council of Ministers, where decisions on financial regulations are taken by qualified majority voting. Outside the EU on the other hand the City would still be able to have access to EU capital markets since this is enshrined in the WTO's General Agreement on Trade and Services (GATS). Its adherence to EU regulations in the past would also mean that the European Securities and Markets Authority (ESMA) would be unable to refuse the UK 'equivalence' status for trading purposes. Thereafter, however, the UK could choose which EU regulations to adopt and could fundamentally change them if she wished as far as the UK was concerned. Parliament could in this way make Britain much more attractive to foreign business. Finally, by reclaiming a seat of her own on key international financial institutions, the UK could gain a more significant say in drafting the international rules that the EU then adopts for its own legislation. Britain would also be able, once free of the EU, to negotiate her own free trade treaties with countries around the world. As Switzerland and Iceland have done already, she could negotiate a free trade treaty with China. She could also negotiate a free trade treaty with India. Attempts by India since 2006 to negotiate a free-trade treaty with the EU have gotten nowhere. Yet Britain is the third largest investor in India and India is the third-largest investor in the UK, owning more here than in the rest of the EU combined. Indian firms who trade with the UK are usually English-speaking, share our commercial and accounting practices and operate according to the same common-law norms and arbitration procedures. Yet in the words of Dan Hannan, the Tory MEP, 'When it comes to trade, though...Britain's natural ties—of language and law, habit and history, culture and kinship—are scrambled by protectionist European tariffs.' An independent Britain would have little difficulty in reaching agreement with India. Her first priority, of course, would be to negotiate that free trade treaty with the EU, something which would be in the interest of both parties.

Altogether, therefore, British industry and the City have nothing to fear from Brexit. The losers would be those large international law and consultancy firms that at present make a fortune arguing over every dot and comma of EU regulations and contracts; those multinationals who use their large HR and legal departments and lobbyists to influence EU legislation in such a way as to exclude smaller firms and rivals; and those international corporations who make 'sweetheart deals' in one EU state to disadvantage tax collection in others. Political losers would be those European romantics who confuse the internationally powerless, domestically undemocratic and fraudulent reality of the EU with some benign federalist utopia that brings peace and democracy. Their illusion will only begin to shatter when the brutal fact of Britain's exit at last confronts them.

Returning to the positive side, Brexit would also allow Britain to ditch the Common Agricultural Policy, the Common Fishing Policy (and thereby regain control of her territorial waters) as well as all other EU policies which Parliament could replace by ones designed to suit British national interests. There would be no longer any need to worry about EU institutions such as the European Council, the Council of Ministers, the Commission, the Court of Justice, or the various EU agencies controlling everything from police to foreign policy. European citizenship would be replaced by British citizenship once again and European passports would be replaced by UK passports as in the past. The EU flag and anthem would become symbols of a friendly, neighbouring but now foreign state, albeit probably one in dissolution. The United Kingdom, in short, would once again become a self-governing democracy with a government elected by and directly accountable to the British people and no one else. English and Scots law would be supreme and no longer subordinated to European law which would revert to being foreign.

Clearly by withdrawing from the EU, Britain would in no sense be isolated or vulnerable. She would still be Europe's leading military power, despite the Defence Review of 2010, and still one of only 5 or 6 nations able to project power across the globe. Indeed, in terms of defence and foreign policy, her departure would, to put it mildly, create substantially greater problems for the EU than for the UK, leaving France in defence and intelligence matters, the only real player in the whole EU. Britain would also remain one of only a handful of nuclear armed nations and one of perhaps only five in possession of sophisticated launch and range capabilities. British forces would remain strategic assets whether one includes those based in Cyprus playing a key role in intelligence gathering in the Middle East or her highly regarded SAS (special forces) and intelligence gathering networks across the globe. She would still have a special relationship with the USA, a seat on the Security Council of the UNO, and a have a key voice in 96—yes, 96!--different international organizations including important ones such as the Bank for International Settlements, the Commonwealth of Nations, the Council of Europe, the G5, the G8, the G20, the IMF, NATO, OECD, the UN, the United Nations Economic Commission for Europe, the UN Security Council, the WHO and the WTO.

Renewed independence would also mean that Britain would once again control her borders and therefore control immigration.

Today, according to opinion polls, this is the topic which concerns British people most. In the period from 1991 to 2014 it increased by 95%, from 329,000 to 632,000. Emigration also increased—by 13%--but taking the two together, according to figures from the House of Commons Library published in September 2015, net immigration grew from an annual average of 37,000 in the period 1991-1995 to an average of 232,000 in the period 2010 to 1014. In June 2015, according to the latest figures, net immigration reached 336,000, up 82,000 from 2014. Of these, 183,000 were from the EU (a rise of 53,000 over the previous year) and of these EU immigrants, 53,000 were from Romania and Bulgaria, almost double the 28,000 who arrived during the previous year. Only 61% of immigrants from the EU had jobs to go to.

These are remarkable figures, since according to Migration Watch, were this trend to continue, the British population will soar by eight million over the next 15 years, with 68% of that rise due to immigration. By 2029, in this scenario, the population will have increased by the quite unsustainable equivalent of the populations of Glasgow, Oxford, Birmingham, Manchester, Sheffield, Leeds, Bradford and Bristol combined.

The rise in immigration has led to a very heated debate in the UK. Firstly, it is disputed whether this is a good or bad thing. Among the cosmopolitan elite in London, the multinational culture of Britain's capital city is held to have been culturally and economically enriched by the arrival of young, ambitious, often well-educated and multilingual foreigners whose drive and initiative spur on London's economy. Both the Treasury and business in general appear to regard immigration as an unalloyed benefit and according to Caroline Fairbairn, head of the CBI, immigration constitutes a boost to the British economy. Yet, according to *Times* columnist Melanie Philips (4 December 2015), 'This is the most myopic short-termism. Businesses and the Treasury view immigrants as workers paying taxes. But such people may have dependants; and they also grow older, thus taking more out of the economy as they put in. This is quite apart from the impact on housing, education and social services which are unable to cope with these numbers. That's why in 2008 the Lords Economic Affairs Committee said it found no evidence that net immigration produced significant economic benefits.' Academic opinion remains divided. Meanwhile, outside London, the increase in size of the lower sections of the labour force is held to depress wages and employment prospects.

There is, however, another dispute about the rise in immigration. According to some political inside sources, it has occurred because first New Labour and subsequently David Cameron's Conservative government deliberately encouraged it for political reasons. Andrew Neather, now a journalist with the London *Evening Standard*, but previously a political adviser to Tony Blair, Jack Straw and David Blunkett, wrote in an article in his newspaper in October 2009, that New Labour had opened the economy to mass immigration not simply for economic motives but to socially engineer a truly multicultural country and to 'rub the Right's nose in diversity'. The policy change originated apparently after the publication of a policy paper from the Performance and Innovation Unit, a think-tank based in 10 Downing Street. The policy lasted till almost 2009 and brought in some 2.3 million migrants to Britain. According to Neather, New Labour took pains not to discuss the shift in policy publicly out of fear of alienating its core working-class vote. Presumably the assumption was that immigrants would vote Labour. As for Cameron's Conservatives, their stated policy before the 2010 and 2015 general elections was to bring down net migration to a figure 'in the tens of thousands'. Clearly they spectacularly failed to do so, yet according to Nick Timothy, former political chief of staff to Tory Home Secretary, Theresa May, this was just propaganda. George Osborne's spending review of November 2015 showed that the Chancellor's plans depend on migration adding at least 185,000 to the population each year and according to Timothy, increasing immigration numbers make the Treasury's balance sheet look healthier. In his words in the blog Conservativehome published on 1 December 2015: '...there is a new reason why the Treasury is keener than ever on mass immigration. It might not bring any significant economic benefits for existing British citizens, but it does mean a bigger population, and a bigger population means a bigger economy overall, which means that the effects of spending cuts increases when the deficit is measured as a percentage of GDP. In the past, the Treasury has sought to inflate its way out of economic trouble. These days it takes a similar approach—not just by artificially increasing the money supply but by inflating the size of the population: quantitative easing meets demographic loosening...The trouble is, as the Autumn Statement made plain last week, other than in the Home office, the Government is no longer trying to cut net migration—and we can expect the numbers to keep going up and up.' An already bitter debate on immigration has been made even more intense, therefore, by these interventions. People who oppose immigration are convinced that their political leaders are not telling them the truth. This has made it even more imperative in the prime minister's mind to be seen to reach some sort of victory on immigration— however cosmetic—over the EU.

So far, however, his negotiations with the EU have demonstrated conclusively that there is little he can do about immigration. The principle of free movement of people remains inviolable as far as other EU leaders are concerned and they believe his aim of refusing in-work benefits to EU migrants for their first four years in the UK would be illegal under EU law. Since the rest of his negotiating demands are clearly trivial, he himself has declared that his stance on immigration must be met. On the other hand that stance is rather illogical. By promising a 'living wage' of £9 a week to all workers in the UK by 2020, he has created a much greater incentive for EU migrants to enter Britain than any in-work benefits they might (but usually do not) apply for. Clearly the only solution to his problem is to take Britain out of the EU altogether. Thereafter the UK could have a proper debate about immigration and Parliament alone could devise a policy designed to suit British interests that would be supported by the British people.

The migrant crisis in continental Europe discussed in the previous chapter, however, makes Cameron's present difficulties look miniscule. Should two or three million migrants be accepted into the EU with their dependants, in a few years' time, between eight and twenty million new EU citizens would have the right to enter Britain. According to a report in the *Times* of 16 July 2015, there has already been a 'surge' in migrants entering [Britain] by the back door: 'Thousands of non-European migrants have arrived in Britain having earlier gained citizenship in other EU countries, according to a report published today. Many were from India, South Africa, Brazil and Sri Lanka, as well as Canada and the United States...Overall the number of EU citizens living in the UK who were born outside the union rose from 78,000 in 2004 to 264,000 at the beginning of this year, according to the report by the University of Oxford's Migration Observatory.' Migrants from Portugal made up almost a fifth of the total, followed by Italy on 36,000, France 33,000 and Spain, 30,000. Migration Watch UK commented: 'The numbers have almost trebled in ten years. The issuing of passports is the responsibility of individual EU countries. These passports carry with them the full right to free movement. It follows that this increased flow could become a back door to Britain. So this is another case for strong controls on EU migration to Britain.' Yet, given the present EU migrant crisis, possibly millions of migrants accepted today by Germany, Sweden and other EU states could enter Britain by precisely this back door in just a few years' time.

Should Turkey become a member state, yet another 75-80 million would acquire the right of free entry, not by the back door but by the front door. Most of these immigrants, of course, would be Muslims, very few of them terrorists of course; still, if they arrived in huge numbers, they would inevitably pose a formidable challenge to preserving Britain's traditional way of life. Brexit alone offers the UK an opportunity to escape these European problems. The situation of British citizens living in the EU and EU citizens living in the UK would, of course, have to be addressed in the light of such an eventuality. Fortunately, there would be no need for any sudden exodus of either group and neither would find themselves in the position of illegal immigrants overnight as one Europhile Tory MP has suggested. The 1969 Vienna Convention on the Law of Treaties, which has articles on 'acquired rights' would take effect. These rights are built up by individuals over time and remain in force despite subsequent treaties signed by their national governments. They were acknowledged when Greenland withdrew from the EEC when, employing the term 'vested rights' the EU Commission declared that Greenland would retain the 'substance' of free movement rights of EU workers at the time of withdrawal. The Vienna Convention also makes provision for a 'transitional period' and this, too, would prevent any government from deporting migrants. Meanwhile any independent British government could negotiate an amicable solution to any difficulties.

The real case for Brexit, however, is not the knowledge that industry and the City would benefit from it or that migration could be controlled, but as already stated, that Britain could reclaim its position as an independent, self-governing democracy with a government directly and solely responsible to its elected representatives. In chapter two, the success of this system in previous centuries was traced and once Brexit occurs, it is a success story that can be resumed. Britain should reclaim her independence because she is a highly successful country with global influence and has absolutely no need to submit to the rules and regulations of a declining, incompetent and fraudulent EU bureaucracy run by failed, superannuated, political nonentities. National pride alone should make this clear.

If the British seem perennially reluctant to acknowledge their success, others notice the scope of their achievements. Recently the UK has hosted a very successful Olympic Games, Commonwealth Games and is home to the English Premier League which is a truly global big business. Its teams have devoted fans all over the world. But Britain also hosts world-class cricket matches at Lords, grand-slam tennis at Wimbledon, rugby at Twickenham, Murrayfield, Cardiff Arms Park, is home in golf to the Open, and in horse-racing to the Grand National and Ascot, not to mention Formula One, athletics, cycling and rowing. In 2015 she secured world champions in Formula One, tennis and boxing. Other nations do host similarly prestigious events but no other country can claim such a deep and diverse heritage hosting so many top events. In high culture she has world-class orchestras, opera houses, theatre companies, dance companies. Her film actors are world stars and her television programmes are exported all over the world. Indeed, the Office of National Statistics demonstrated with data from 2012 that the creative industries in Britain accounted for 5.2% of the economy (£71.4 billion Gross Value Added) and provided 1.68 million jobs. Moreover, this area of activity was growing at 10% per annum. The BBC still enjoys the strongest brand name in world broadcasting while Sky is also a global leader and innovator in digital TV. As for the 'little platoons' made so famous by Edmund Burke, Ewen Stewart has commented: 'What other country has so many diverse interest groups from the Royal Society for the Protection of Birds to the National Trust while founding OXFAM and Amnesty International for example?' British universities are also world leaders. The *Times* annual league table of world universities always demonstrates the dominance of the Anglo-sphere with a staggering 124 of the top 200 universities coming from the USA, UK, Australia, Canada and New Zealand. Britain's share at 31 puts in a clear second place behind the USA. The UK also has six out of the top ten European universities, with Oxford, Cambridge, Imperial College, LSE and UCL being global brand names. Britain is also second to the USA in the number of Nobel Prizes gained. At the elite level of education, therefore, Britain performs quite disproportionately to its size of population. And elite education is big business these days. Britain is also a world leader in musical festivals, another billion pound sector of the economy. Almost 40,000 jobs are now sustained by the British music festival industry and in 2014 no fewer than 9.5 million people attended these events. 550,000 tourists even travelled to Britain to take part in them. Glastonbury now hosts 200,000 people annually, the Cambridge Folk Festival, 10,000. Tickets for Glastonbury cost £225 this year but were sold out in 25 minutes. According to Liam Halligan, the economics editor of the *Sunday Telegraph*, on 2 August 2015, 'British music is legendary around the world, holding a unique place in the development of rock and pop, with UK artists still accounting for one in seven of all albums sold.' The UK's broader creative industries sector, according to Halligan, is today worth £80 billion annually. One reason for the growth of such industry may be that Britain, according to the annual Prosperity Index is the best economy in the EU in which to start a business. In its annual report for 2015, the Legatum Institute, which publishes the Index, said that 88 per cent of Britons now believe that if you work hard you can get ahead (up from 78 per cent in 2010). According to the Institute, 'The UK is among the most prosperous countries in the world. This is due to a number of factors including the a firm belief in the rule of law, the ability to protect its citizens, and the fact that it is one of the most open and free nations in the world.' It also pointed out that the UK economy is growing faster than that of any other major EU country and added: 'The gap is full-time employment between the richest and poorest 20pc of the country has halved since 2009. This is the biggest turnaround of any major developed economy.' (Report in the *Daily Telegraph* of 2 November 2015) Britain, too, is at the centre of the growth of alternative finance (alt-fi) in Europe according to a recent report by the Cambridge Centre for Alternative Finance. Much of this involves on-line platform-based finance and in Europe this grew by 146% each year between 2012 and 2014. Funding to consumers, entrepreneurs, renewable energy projects, community organisations and good causes across the EU rose from 487 million euros in 2012 to 2.96 billion euros in 2014 and may have surpassed seven billion euros in 2015. Yet at the centre of this development was the UK, which alone accounted for three-quarters of all that funding—the remaining members contributing 25.7 per cent. In 2014 UK alt-fi processed 2.33 billion euros of deals compared with the mere 154 million euros financed in Germany, the second placed member state. On a per capita basis, that is 36 euros in the UK compared to merely 1.7 euros in Germany. (Report in the *Times* of 8 December 2015)

All this may explain why the Global Influence Index compiled by Portland Communications and Facebook puts Britain at the top of its list for 'soft power' influence, ahead of Germany, the United States, France, Canada, Australia, Switzerland, Netherlands, Denmark and Italy. (China is consigned to the basement.) Britain's cultural power is credited with more international chart-topping music albums than any other country. The foreign following of British football teams is in a league of its own, while it is home to 29 Unesco World Heritage sites. The UK also scores highly in areas such as 'engagement with the world' with visa-free travel to 174 countries and its diplomats staffing the largest number of permanent missions. The index also shows that Britain does well on education, attracting vast numbers of foreign students, with its universities second only to America's. (See report in the *Times*, 16 July, 2015)

So why should anyone believe that Britain should not be independent? There is every indication that outside the EU Britain would have just a distinguished future as she had before she entered that dysfunctional and undemocratic body. Given her wealth, her enterprise, her freedoms, her democratic traditions, her hard and soft power, her history, there is surely no alternative. It is now time for Britain to leave the European Union. The forthcoming referendum offers her that chance.

***

Appendix: The EU and its Decline: A Factual Explanation

What is the European Union all about? Should British citizens vote to stay in or get out when they cast their ballots in Britain's forthcoming referendum on EU membership? Why indeed did Britain join the EU in the first place and what if anything has she gained from being a member of it? These are the main questions discussed above in this book, which has been written by a liberal academic, whose speciality is European history and politics and who concludes that British voters should choose to quit the EU.

For readers totally unacquainted with the EU and its structures, aims and modes of operation, this appendix is provided as a guide as well as an account of its most recent history.

What exactly is the European Union? It is not an easy organization to describe. Its hybrid constitution includes among other bodies a decision-making European Council (summit meetings of the heads of government of the 28 member states), a powerful bureaucracy run by the European Commission with thirty-odd departments (directorates-general), a Parliament that discusses Commission proposals, and a Supreme Court (the European Court of Justice) to rule on disputes. The Commission has its own President as does the Council. One Commissioner heads the new EU Foreign Service and there is also a separate organization—the Eurozone-- for the 19 member states who employ the would-be "single currency" of the EU, the euro. 9 member states, including Britain, however, use their own currencies. The governance of the Eurozone does not relate intelligibly to the other institutions previously described. Indeed, in the recent crisis over Greek debt, its governance seems to have been given over to a hybrid body known as the 'troika' representing the European Commission, the European Central Bank and the International

Monetary Fund. This has no constitutional basis in European law. Another body supervising the negotiations with Greece has been the 'Eurogroup', which also has its own President. It is supposed to be composed of the finance ministers of all Eurozone member states but when the Greek finance minister in 2015 at a crucial point in the negotiations over Greece's debt objected to being excluded from the Eurogroup and asked for legal justification for this, he was told: 'Well, the Eurogroup does not exist in law. There is no treaty which has convened this group.' Varoufakis, the Greek minister concerned, later commented in an interview in the *New Statesman*: 'So what we have is a non-existent group that has the greatest power to determine the lives of Europeans. It's not answerable to anyone, given that it does not exist in law, no minutes are kept; and it's confidential...so no citizen ever knows what is said within...These are decisions of almost life and death, and no member has to answer to anybody.' As explained in the main text, this is true of much of EU governance (the Council operates in secret as do Commission committees) and is part of the EU's notorious 'democratic deficit' explained in more detail above. Yet the lament of Jykri Katainen, the Finnish Vice-President of the European Commission in charge of jobs, growth, investment and competitiveness, that 'we don't change our policy according to elections' was widely quoted during the Greek crisis—as if anyone had ever suggested otherwise. Meanwhile, another problem for Varoufakis during the crisis was that (according to the President of France in particular) no country is allowed to abandon the euro. Membership of the Eurozone is irreversible. Hence, for making contingency plans for Greece to return to the drachma, Varoufakis was at one point considered liable to be charged with high treason!

What is the purpose of the EU? What is the aim of the continuing waves of European integration, the succession of treaties concluded by member states and the goal of 'ever-closer union' laid down in the founding treaty of the EU, the Treaty of Rome.

One way of finding out is to consult a document from the Official Publications of the European Union whose English-language title is *European Unification. The Origins and Growth of the European Community*. Several editions are available in different languages but I will now quote from the third edition of 1989 which appears to be a translation from the German by someone called Klaus-Dieter Borchardt. The section headed 'Political Integration' opens as follows: 'Although the principles and measures laid down in the Treaties relate only to the establishment and operation of the common market, *economic integration is not meant to be an end in itself but merely an intermediate stage on the road to political integration.*' [author's emphasis] It is imperative for British voters to bear this in mind when the YES camp during referendum debates talks exclusively—as it will—about economic statistics or the Single Market. The ultimate aim of the EU according to its own official publication is *political* NOT economic integration. The document then quite rightly explains that political integration can come about by either 'confederalist' or 'federalist' methods. The confederalist one is then rather dismissed in the sentence: 'This is the principle underlying the work of the Council of Europe and the OECD'— obviously inadequately European institutions since they preserve the autonomy of member states. The document instead reserves its enthusiasm for the federalist approach:

'The federalist approach, on the other hand, aims to dissolve the traditional distinctions between Nation States. The outdated notion of inviolable and indivisible national sovereignty gives way to the view that the imperfections of social and international co-existence, the specific shortcomings of the nation State system and the dangers of the predominance of one State over others (so frequent a phenomenon in European history) can only be overcome by individual States pooling their sovereignty under a supranational community.

The result is a European federation in which the common destiny of its peoples—still retaining their individual identities—is guided, and their future assured by common (federal) authorities.

The European Community is a product of this federalist approach, though in a somewhat modified form owing to the Member States' reluctance simply to abandon altogether their sovereignty and the old nation State structure which they had only just regained and consolidated after the Second World War in favour of a European federation. Once again a compromise had to be found which, without necessarily establishing a federal structure, would provide more than mere cooperation along confederal lines. The solution, both brilliant and simple was to seek to bridge the gap between national autonomy and European federation in a gradual process. Rather than relinquish all sovereignty overnight, the Member States were asked merely to abandon the dogma of indivisibility.'

This seems a perfectly acceptable description of the process of 'ever-closer union' at work before 1989. The political independence of member states ('all sovereignty') is to disappear completely, but gradually, not 'overnight'. (The first President of the European Commission, Walter Hallstein, wrote a book on European integration entitled *Der unvollendete Bundesstaat* or 'The uncompleted Federal State'. Its official title in English was *Europe in the Making*.)

There are three points to note regarding the pamphlet. First, since 1989, thanks to a number of further treaties, the EU has made substantial progress towards becoming a completely federal state. It has acquired a foreign service, an intelligence service, a police service, EU arrest warrants, a single legal personality and the absorption of the European Council into the treaty structure making that body accountable to the European Court. It even asks members to give forewarning of any desire to secede from the Union so as to precipitate negotiations. In short (through the Lisbon Treaty which came into force in 2009) it now has its own constitution. Ironically, its desire seems to be to become just a large nation state like its perceived international rivals Russia,

China and the United States. It has its own passport, anthem, flag, parliament, constitution, currency, police force, diplomatic service, supreme court, civil service, intelligence service, laws and policies. All it lacks to be a fully modern state is an elected government, armed forces and a single tax system. One should add, of course, democratic accountability and legitimacy.

Perhaps the point made above about its acquisition of the various trappings of a conventional nation-state needs to be stressed. Despite the dreamers in the pro-European camp, the EU clearly has no notion of 'post-national' politics. It represents no vision of a new international order. It merely sees itself as a new, but—crucially—bigger nation state, desperate to promote an artificial European nationalism through symbols and especially propaganda. This is absolutely vital for few if any people in Europe wave EU flags about at football matches or popular gatherings. There is no European nation or *demos* on which to base a European nation-state or democracy. Hence the observations of that keenest and most celebrated of European commentators, Timothy Garten Ash of Oxford University and the *Guardian*, writing in that newspaper on 10 July 2015: 'European democracy remains national, and behind that truth is an ever deeper fact: there is hardly any more of a European public sphere today than when I started studying Europe 40 years ago. There is a thin layer of publications that reach a small, educated audience across the continent, but most people still get the bulk of their news and views from national media— even when there is a shared language. In Vienna recently I was told how much of Austrian coverage of Greece differed in tone from that in Germany.' He continued: ' "Among a people without fellow-feeling, especially if they read and speak different languages," wrote John Stuart Mill, "the united public opinion necessary to the working of representative government cannot exist." Europe has yet to prove him wrong. I have been in six European countries over the past six weeks, and the lack of fellow-feeling between them has been painful to observe.' His comments explain the EU's obsession with propaganda and self-promotion, not to mention its desperate, almost pathetic, yet constant attempts to justify itself. The more these attempts to manufacture an artificial European nationalism fail (*pace* Garton Ash) the more money it spends trying to succeed. Today the EU spends over £500 million annually promoting itself and produces thousands of publications, videos, and information campaigns to do this. Its advertising budget is larger than Coca Cola's. The budget of the Commission's Directorate-General for Communications is actually larger than that of its Directorate-General for the Budget, which employs less than half the staff of the former. The Directorate-General for Trade employs only two-thirds as many staff. Much of the EU's propaganda, sadly, is directed at indoctrinating schoolchildren—no doubt on the Jesuit model. For example, the Official Publications Office publishes children's comic books in order to extol the virtues of the EU in primary schools. According to the Brussels correspondent of the *Daily Telegraph* (10 August 2015) a comic published in 2000 to promote EU aid work cost £200,000. Another comic book, entitled *On the Road to Victory,* was commissioned by the EU Directorate-General for the Budget and has a teacher tell a schoolboy: 'What we must remember is that money that countries invest in the European Union is more useful to all its citizens than if each country spent it individually.' It is available in 23 different languages. North Korean schools may yet want to adapt if not adopt it.

EU propaganda reaches practically everywhere. For example, in the introduction to his latest work on the EU, *The European Union. An Obituary* (Verso, 2016), the distinguished historian, Professor John D. Gillingham III, now at the Centre for European Studies at Harvard University, states: 'Directly or indirectly the European Union has funded the bulk of the scholarly literature written about it...The many scholars, commentators, associated experts and like-minded journalists, who have spent careers doing EU research are nearly all devotees of the Euro-cult.' According to the *Sunday Telegraph* of *25 October 2015*, even the BBC was discovered to have been the beneficiary of EU funds: 'BBC's Media Action (the broadcaster's charitable arm) was paid £9.3 million between 2011 and 2014, much of it to deliver the EU's European Neighbourhood Policy. As part of this work, BBC Media Action led a consortium of media companies under a three-year project which provided training for hundreds of journalists in 17 countries on the outskirts of Europe.' Reporters in the scheme attended 'study tours to the EU in Brussels' during which they were able to interview 'top EU policy makers'. The federalist message is spread assiduously.

The EU clearly wants to unite a continent in the same way that nineteenth-century Italian nationalists united a peninsula. And just as they wanted Italy to become a great power, the leaders of the EU would like Europe to become a superpower holding the balance between Russia, the USA and China. Horst Teltschik, the chief foreign policy adviser to the German Chancellor Helmut Kohl used to argue that there should be a world balance of power and that maintaining this is the role of the EU, even though, rather pathetically, it is in relative economic decline, has no armed forces and has a pacifist outlook. Certainly, its legacy in international affairs is pacifism not peace. According to the Pew Research Centre, for example, a majority of Germans would refuse to fight to defend Poland or the Baltic States. Nor do EU states seem interested in defence. For example, on 5 August 2015, the Scottish *Daily Record* under the headline 'Bang out of order for Dutch army' reported that 'soldiers are making their own "bang, bang" noises during training because they have no bullets.

The Dutch army have been hit by an ammunition shortage and it is feared the playground-like situation could dent morale. Retired Major-General Harm de Jonge said the matter was "extremely serious".' A Dutch government, it will be recalled, fell from power in 2002 as a result of a damning report into the failure of Dutch troops to protect 8,000 Bosnian Muslim men and boys in Srebrenica from being massacred by Bosnian Serbs in 1995 in the worst single atrocity of the Bosnian war. Continuing the theme of a lack of interest in defence, in September 2014 a German parliamentary report leaked to the German press and obtained by the *Washington Post* revealed that only one of Germany's four submarines was operational, that only 70 out of its 180 Boxer tanks were fit for deployment, and that just seven out of the navy's fleet of 43 helicopters were flightworthy. Operations in Africa and Afghanistan had also broken down due to helicopter malfunctions. Such, according to the report, was the shocking state of Germany's military hardware. All in all, therefore, despite its size, the EU possesses neither international weight nor democratic institutional coherence. One is reminded of Bismarck's jibe about Italy: 'It has a large appetite but poor teeth.' Its foreign policy record is examined in more detail in the main text.

Supporters of British membership of the EU, although reluctant to acknowledge either its democratic deficit or lack of international influence, do recognise the significance of its political and constitutional evolution, albeit inadvertently. Their mantra in debates is always: 'to trade with Europe, you have to be part of Europe.' Economically, however, this is bizarre. No one says 'to trade with China you have to be part of China'. That would be very scary indeed. No one has suggested that in order to trade with the USA we have to adopt the dollar as our currency or become the fifty-first state. Nor do we require a federal union or common currency in order to trade with Japan. Yet

Europhiles insist that in order to trade with the EU we must retain our European passports and citizenship, obey European laws, be represented in the European Parliament, be represented by the EU diplomatic service and that we must obey the judgements of the European Court. All of this is proof that EU membership is far from being an ordinary commercial relationship. Or in the words of the officially authorized EU pamphlet quoted above, economic integration is just an 'intermediate stage' *en route* to *political* union.

The debate in the referendum therefore should not concentrate on economics or the Single Market. To trade with China, you do not have to be part of China, to trade with the USA, you do not have to be part of the USA, to trade with Japan you do not have to be part of Japan. To trade with the EU you do not have to be part of the EU. We can do this from the outside as a normal, self-governing, independent democracy just as other countries—the USA, Japan, Canada, Australia and New Zealand—do.

The second point that arises from the official pamphlet quoted above is the nature of national sovereignty. People get confused about this. It is not about power. Zimbabwe, for example, is bankrupt and has no power internationally but is most certainly a sovereign state. If you enter Zimbabwe and break its laws you will be dealt with very severely. Why? Because inside Zimbabwe, legal authority, however arbitrarily applied, lies with the government of Zimbabwe, which has the final authority to deal with you. No other authority can override it. So sovereignty is about final legal authority. Someone must have the authority to make a final decision on a policy and in Britain this is Parliament (strictly speaking the Queen in Parliament). This sovereignty by dint of its finality may be delegated but cannot be 'pooled' or 'shared'. And what is delegated by Parliament can always be reclaimed by Parliament or by the British people if Parliament delegates its final legal authority to it in a referendum. This is what is at stake in the referendum on EU membership. Should Britain insist on controlling its own sovereignty through Parliament? Or should it allow the federalist process of 'ever-closer union' to continue to the stage where Parliament will no longer be able to exercise its sovereignty at all, as is the aim of European integration as the EU's own pamphlet makes clear? Some will argue that, outside the Eurozone, and with the few cosmetic concessions that the EU will inevitably throw to David Cameron as a political life-line, there is no threat to British sovereignty. This, however, would be a grave mistake. Despite the travails of the Eurozone recently, there are, incredibly, still voices in Britain calling for us to join the euro—Richard Branson, Paddy Ashdown, Michael Heseltine, and Tony Blair for example. And European integration is rather like a vampire. Every time it seems safely buried, it rises from the dead—leading to yet another treaty with more regulations and red tape and still greater EU authority over nation states. Since the Treaty of Rome (1957) there has been the Single European Act (1986), the Maastricht Treaty (1992), the Amsterdam Treaty (1997), the Nice Treaty (2001), the Constitutional Treaty (2005) and the Lisbon Treaty (2007). And on 22 June 2015, the Commission President produced the 'Report of the Five Presidents' (those of the EU's Commission, Council, Eurogroup, Parliament and Central Bank) which mapped out a blueprint for a full-blown Euro-area super-state by 2025 with Britain in an outer tier of EU members but 'still affected by the move to deeper integration,' according to a *Sunday Times* report of 20 August 2015. The same report quoted Valdis Dombrovskis, the commissioner in charge of implementing the proposals as stating: 'Until mid-2017 we can do without legislative changes. Then we will set up a group, which should come up with proposals that might eventually require treaty changes.' The only way, therefore, to avoid the process of 'ever-closer union' completely destroying our independence is to quit the EU entirely. If David Cameron emerges from negotiations with the EU claiming he has a legal protocol, a binding promise, or some other diplomatic instrument removing any obligation on the part of the UK to pursue 'ever-closer union', pay no attention to it. It will be meaningless. The only true guarantee of retaining our national sovereignty and the supremacy of Parliament is to quit the EU altogether. EU promises cannot be trusted. The federalist vampire always rises from the dead and according to Dombrovskis, quoted above, it is already stirring in its grave. Indeed, President Hollande of France, according to a report in the *Daily Telegraph* of 8 October 2015, while outlining yet more federalist plans to the European Parliament to cope with the EU's current migrant crisis, plans that included a common defence policy and a shared asylum system and coast guard—and this only one day after the British Home Secretary, Theresa May had declared she would 'not in a thousand years' agree to such a common asylum system—told British MEPs: 'If [you] don't want to strengthen Europe, then there's only one road...the road for those who are not convinced of Europe [is] to leave Europe.' He added: 'There is no other way. It's a horrible path, but it's a logical path. Leave Europe...' According to the report, Hollande's remarks reflected 'mounting frustration in Paris at Mr. Cameron's determination to get an "a la carte Europe". Many French government officials think Britain already holds more than enough opt-outs on key pieces of policy and are exasperated by its demands for more.' Yet Hollande's position was clear: Britain should accept more federalism or quit the EU.

The third point which arises from the pamphlet is its claim that federalism prevents one member state from dominating the others. Clearly this is untrue. For a few decades from the 1960s France and Germany ran the show in tandem much as Austria and Hungary between 1867 and 1918 ran the

Habsburg Monarchy. But the Franco-German dualism is no more. Germans, like everyone else, are quite aware who now rules the EU roost.

Not long before he became German Kaiser, the future Wilhelm II, still Crown Prince of the Hohenzollerns, visited his ally Austria-Hungary. While in Vienna he had sex with a prostitute, who, afterwards was interrogated (one is tempted to say 'debriefed') by the Habsburg intelligence services. The girl explained that Wilhelm had evinced no determination to take control of Austria; Austria, rather, would fall into Germany's lap like ripe fruit in the not-too-distant future. This was held to be inevitable. And Austria did fall under German control during the First World War and later as a result of the *Anschluss* of 1938.

Today Germany finds herself in control of the EU. Perhaps this was never her intention—the introduction of the single currency after all was intended by the French to control a newly-united Germany. Still, the fact of German dominance has been ruthlessly exposed by German diplomacy during the Greek crisis. Indeed, one of Angela Merkel's colleagues, Volker Kauder, the leader of Ms Merkel's conservatives in the German parliament, delighted his party's conference in November 2011 by boasting: 'Suddenly Europe is speaking German.' He added: 'Not in the language but in the acceptance of the instruments for which Angela Merkel fought for so long and so successfully.' The former German foreign secretary and leader of Germany's Greens, Joschka Fischer, has likewise claimed: 'Germany is and has been the driving force behind European integration.' Germany's leading public intellectual, Jürgen Habermas has even stressed—rather ironically to a non-German—that only Germany is capable of organising European political and fiscal union and that opposition to Eurozone emergency measures led by Germany is tantamount to the kind of populism 'that repeats the errors of 1914'. Marzel Fratzscher, head of the German Institute for Economic Research in Berlin, has said: 'Germany has, at the end of the day, helped determine most of the European decisions of the last five years.' More to the point, Germany's *Stern* magazine in its edition of 17 July 2015 had a picture of Angela Merkel on its front cover under the headline: 'The Ice Queen. How Angela Merkel became the most feared woman in Europe.' The article inside the magazine was headed: 'Dominatrix (*Schmerzdame*). Angela Merkel has taught Europe to fear. Once again the Chancellor has saved Greece, albeit on German conditions. And they are hard, perhaps too hard.'

Perhaps the best analysis of German dominance is the German sociologist, Professor Ulrich Beck's best-seller of 2012, *German Europe,* which begins with the German radio announcement of February 2012: 'Today the German Bundestag will decide the fate of Greece'—which, of course, it has been doing ever since. According to Beck, Greece and other European debtor states have become the 'new underclass' of the EU. He continues: 'They are compelled to acquiesce in their loss of sovereignty and endure blows to their national pride. Furthermore their democratic right to self-determination dwindles to the alternative: acceptance or exit'. In his view, 'the meaning of European cooperation has become fundamentally ambiguous and it is above all the new underclass that is the suffering from this ambiguity. Its fate is uncertain: in the best case, it will be federalism, in the worst neo-colonialism.' Little wonder then that the leader of the Spanish political party Podemos, Pablo Inglesias, has declared: 'We don't want to be a German colony.' Still, it might not be so bad a position to be in. After all, again according to Beck, '(Germans) have become model democrats, model nuclear dropouts, model savers and model pacifists...Measured by its own history, this is the best Germany we have ever had.' So that's alright then! To quote Beck yet again:'...because Germany is the wealthiest country, it has the only real say at the centre of Europe.'

German dominance, however, may not be as permanent as people think. Contemporary Germans may not even relish it themselves, but in any case, Germany has serious problems to face, particularly its fast-shrinking and ageing population. The London *Times* reported on 2 June 2015 that 'the birthrate in Germany has fallen to the lowest in the world as more women delay childbirth to concentrate on their career. Only 8.28 births were recorded for every 1,000 Germans over the past five years....The population of Germany is now 81.1 million, but the German office for national statistics said that by 2060 it would be as low as 67.6 million.' By mid-century Germany will very probably not have the workforce to sustain its generous old-age pensions and other welfare benefits. Its infrastructure is already creaking especially in its depopulated eastern provinces and in the Ruhr. Moreover, its much-vaunted structural reforms introduced by Chancellor Schroeder after 2003 may not have produced the kind of jobs required to keep a modern economy going. According to Beck, 'Roughly half the new jobs which were created are precarious. They are made up of around a million agency jobs, 7.4 million so-called mini-jobs (paying 400 euros per month), and 3 million temporary positions etc. This has led to deeper social divisiveness and a rapid earnings gap between the rich and the poor.' The economics of the euro have benefitted German exporters but workers' wages have hardly improved. Moreover, the debtor economies of the Eurozone are hardly capable of buying sufficient German goods leaving German exports reliant on the now less-than-stable Chinese and other non-European markets. In fact, German exports to China fell by 5% in the first half of 2015, according to the *Financial Times* of 14 September 2015. The longer-term outlook for the German economy, the powerhouse of Europe, may not therefore be very bright and long-term growth in the Eurozone looks like being very modest indeed.

Curiously, despite France's famous obsession with long-term employment contracts—*le contrat à durée indéterminée* –permanent job contracts which made up 25% of all new contracts in 2000, today account for less than 16%. Out of 20 million job contracts signed each year, two-thirds are for less than one month. Young people, immigrants and the lesser skilled are those worse affected by this new 'flexibility'. According to the *Financial Times* of 11 August 2015, France, although 'known for providing workers with some of the most secure contracts, generous health benefits and longest holidays, has tolerated pockets of flexibility to help curb record unemployment of 10%. The crisis has accelerated with the financial crisis and the (EU's) current woes.'

If France, like Germany, is experiencing a rise in the number of temporary job contracts, Portugal, like Germany, is experiencing a demographic crisis. The headline of an article on this subject in the *Financial Times* on 13 August 2015 was 'Catastrophe looms for Portugal as fertility rates fall and population ages'. Its correspondent in Lisbon, Peter Wise, reported that the situation was so bad that one clothing company was paying a bonus of 505 euros—the equivalent of a month's minimum wage—as a 'maternity incentive' to female workers to have a baby. Between 2010 and 2014, Portugal lost 198,000 inhabitants, close to 2 per cent of its population, as the number of deaths exceeded births, emigration rose to levels unseen since the 1960s, and immigration slowed to a trickle. If nothing changes, the worst–case projection of the National Statistics Institute (INE) foresees the population of Portugal dropping from 10.5 million to 6.3 million by 2060, while the number of over-65s for every 100 under-65s – the so-called ageing index—would soar from 131 to 464, the highest in Europe. In less than a generation, according to Eurostat, Portugal will be the EU country with the smallest proportion of children, with the percentage of under-15s falling from 14.6 per cent of the population in 2014 to 11.3 per cent in 2050. The phenomenon of a shrinking yet ageing population is already visible in hundreds of villages throughout the country. Village schools have closed, working-age adults have emigrated, leaving only the elderly. Wise quotes one study which concluded: 'Without a new influx of people, the interior of Portugal will be practically empty in 25 years.' Another report quoted by Wise, which was commissioned by the prime minister's office, concludes that the lack of children threatens the country with 'definitive impoverishment' and would leave Portugal 'unsustainable in terms of economic growth, social security and the welfare state.' According to a report of 4 December 2015 in the *Times*, Spain's population, too, is forecast to fall by over five million over the next fifty years and there are already 2,500 'ghost villages' in the country with no inhabitants. Teruel in eastern Spain now has fewer inhabitants per square kilometre than Lapland. Today, Spain has the tenth oldest population in the world. So Portugal and to a lesser extent Spain-- is facing the same bleak prospects in a few decades as Germany. Moreover, apart from really massive immigration, there is little that a country can do to prevent such demographic forecasts becoming reality. Today, of course, a sudden and massive immigration into Germany—not Spain or Portugal—is underway. However, it has not been planned and the political effects of it are still to be seen.

In Italy the financial crisis has also hit the weakest sections of society but more particularly has exacerbated the notorious economic gap between the North and South of the country. According to Istat, the Italian statistics agency, unemployment in the second quarter of 2015 in south and central Italy was 17.7% and among those under the age of 25, 54% (the latest figure for unemployment in Italy as a whole—June 2015—according to the *Financial*

Times on 13 August 201—is 12.7%, with youth unemployment at a record 44.2%.) The figures for central and south Italy led the mayor of the town of Elmas, close to the Sardinian capital of Cagliari, to invent a programme called *Adesso* Parto ('Now I am leaving') which pays unemployed locals to take intensive English lessons, board a cheap flight and look for jobs outside the country. 12,000 euros were allocated on a first-come first-served basis. Applicants did not need to be educated but had to be out of work, have lived in the town for three years, and to have an income no greater than 15,000 euros a year. They could be aged between 18 and 50. The mayor described the project as 'the last-chance saloon'. The story was reported in the *Guardian* in 2015 by Lizzy Davies. According to the *Financial Times* on 11 August 2015, while Italy's output as a whole contracted by 0.4% in 2014, it fell by 1.3% in the South. Before the crisis in 2009, the gross domestic product per capita of residents in the southern regions was 56.2% of that of Italians elsewhere. By 2014 that share had dropped to 53.7%, the lowest in 25 years. More than 60% of southerners, astonishingly, lived off less than 12,000 euros a year in 2014, against 28.5% in the rest of Italy (another shocking statistic). Not surprisingly, a leading southern figure, the anti-mafia writer Roberto Savaino, (who lives under police protection) wrote an open letter in the leading Italian newspaper, *La Republica*, urging the prime minister to take action and to admit that nothing was being done to end the historic problem of the 'desertification' of the Italian South.. To this rebuke, the young 'reforming', centre-left prime minister of Italy, Matteo Renzi, replied telling southerners to 'stop whining'.

Eastern Europe, meanwhile, has also had a strange record inside the Eurozone. Under the CAP a typical Latvian farmer receives a subsidy of 90 euros per hectare per year. His Greek counterpart receives 650. Bulgaria is the poorest country in the EU with an average per capita annual income of merely 4,800 euros in 2012. Electricity bills eat up a huge part of monthly incomes. Yet the EU insists that 16% of Bulgarian electricity by 2020 will have to be supplied by very expensive renewables. Likewise, an EU directive on the comfort of hens in 2012 increased the price of eggs in the Czech Republic by 100%. Slovakia, meanwhile, had to commit 13 billion euros in financial transfers and loan guarantees to Greek bailout funds. That is more than the annual tax revenues of the Slovak government. Average per capita income in Greece in 2012 after two bailouts was 20,100 euros; in Slovakia the figure was 12,100. An article in the *Wall St. Journal* dated 30 April 2012 was headed *At What Cost EU Membership?* After surveying a variety of data it reached the following rough cost-benefit analysis for the Eastern European membership of the Eurozone:

'What happens when we subtract the explicit costs of EU membership, including the contributions of central and eastern countries to the EU budget from the EU's largesse, including cohesion funds and agricultural subsidies? The net "gain" for Slovakia comes to an average of 77 euros per person per year between 2004 and 2010. It was 102 euros in Poland, 115 euros in Hungary, 66 euros in the Czech republic, 200 euros in Estonia, 183 euros in Latvia and 224in Lithuania.
These figures do not take into account the implicit costs of EU membership arising from trade protectionism and regulation (at least 2,662 euros per person in each country according to the Commission's...figures, not to mention bailouts.'

Matteo Renzi, stung by the open letter to him from Savaino, promised Italian southerners a 'master plan' in the future. This is just the kind of thing that EU federalists are always promising, usually involving more control from Brussels. Some leading federalists—including Martin Schulz, the President of the European Parliament (yet another European president!)—are already talking about a new treaty for fiscal and political union, their own version of a 'master plan' to save the EU. And no doubt the Official Publications Office will produce another comic book to 'inform' Europe's schoolchildren just how wonderful this will be. In reality, however, the EU, whose GDP has still to recover its level of 2008, despite a combination of cheap oil, low interest rates, a depreciated euro and quantitative easing (60 billion euros a month early in 2015, 100 billion by May) does not present a picture of a dynamic economy with a glowing future. Its overall growth rate in the second quarter of 2015 was a mere 1.2%. France flat-lined and the figures for Germany and Italy were poor. Experts forecast even smaller growth for the rest of 2015 and do not rule out a renewed recession. UK growth, meanwhile, is now 5% up on its pre-recession peak, that of the USA over 9% above it.

Whether German domination proves permanent or not, the truth of the EU's significant economic relative decline in the world economy cannot really be disguised. If one takes the 15 countries at the core of the EU—Austria, Belgium, Denmark, Finland, France, Germany, Greece, Ireland, Italy, the Netherlands, Luxembourg, Portugal, Spain, Sweden and the United Kingdom—their average growth in the 1970s registered 3.2%, in the 1980s, 2.5%, in the 1990s, 2.2%, and in the 2000s, 1.2%. In 2012 the figure was 1%. 'Europe has been falling back for decades,' states the Wall St. Journal, on the basis of these and other figures. For example, while the US share of global GDP has remained stable for two generations at around 26%, the EU-15's has fallen from almost 35% in 1970 to 26% in 2012. It is expected to keep on falling. Before the advent of the euro, of course, European states in economic difficulty could simply devalue their currencies. Thus from 1980 till the launch of the euro in 1999, the Italian lira and Portuguese escudo lost 108% and 244% of their value against the US dollar respectively. Greece actually devalued the drachma 583% against the dollar from 1981 until its euro entry in January 2001.The deutsche mark meanwhile remained remarkably stable against the dollar, gaining a mere 1.74% over 20 years.

The advent of the euro was supposed to bring economic stability and growth to the EU. Lord Wallace, now leader of the hundreds of Liberal Democratic peers marooned in the House of Lords but formerly an academic specialising in European integration, wrote in 1997: *'Economic logic* made for moves towards a single currency.' However, most leading economists at the time—particularly US Nobel prize winners—thought the scheme intellectually misconceived from the start. The EU was not an 'optimum currency area' and it would prove impossible to coordinate the economies of so many diverse countries. The whole thing was a political initiative masquerading as an economic one. Martin Feldstein—formerly head of the board of US presidential economic advisers and himself a Nobel laureate—argued in a famous article in the *Economist*, that Europe would be better served with more currencies rather than one. In spite of this, the Maastricht Treaty of 1992 had set the stage for Economic and Monetary Union (EMU) and had set down the entry criteria for countries adopting the single currency at 3% for national deficits and 60% of GDP for national debt ratios.

The Eurozone members however paid scant attention to their own rules. The fudging began even before the launch of the euro when in 1998 Italy and Belgium were allowed to enter the currency bloc despite debt-to GDP ratios of almost 120%--almost twice the Maastricht criterion. Italy, indeed had met the annual deficit target of 3% but only by a series of one-off budgetary tricks. France, however, was adamant that all the founding members of the EU should be allowed to join. The pattern was repeated in 2000 when Greece—'the land of Plato'—became the twelfth member despite a debt to GDP ratio in excess of 120%. Supposedly this was on a downward trend, while the 3% target for the national deficit was supposedly met. Then in 2003 both Germany (yes, Germany!) and France became the first countries officially to breach the

Eurozone's 3% deficit ceiling and successfully fought off calls for them to be sanctioned, thus rendering the budget rules a dead letter. In 2004 the European Court of Justice ruled that the European Council had acted outside its authority in sanctioning the breach but its ruling had no effect. In 2005 the European Council then repeated its precedent by allowing Greece's excessive deficits to stand and weakened the rules even further by formal intergovernmental agreement. It could hardly complain, therefore, when in 2009 Athens revealed it had been cooking the books for years and that its expected deficit for   that year would be12.5% of GDP and not the expected one of 3.7%. By May 2012 the Eurozone was again tearing up its rule-book by ignoring the no-bailout clause of the Maastricht Treaty to bail out Greece (for the second time). Then the European Central Bank, which was barred from financing the deficits of member countries, began buying up the bonds of member states in the secondary markets. Later the Bank would tear up its own rules by promising to do anything required to save the euro and start a programme of quantitative easing. By 2012 the Eurozone had acquired a new Fiscal Pact to reassert some order but just a day later Spain flouted its rules on deficit targets without any sanctions being imposed.

Today, the Eurozone, having already bailed out Portugal, Ireland and Cyprus, is in the midst of negotiations with Greece over a third bailout having humiliated that country and its leaders in excruciating financial negotiations. These secured agreement from a left-wing government in Greece (elected on an explicit anti-austerity platform and backed by an overwhelming anti-austerity vote in a national referendum), to implement severe austerity programmes dictated and supervised by the Eurozone, led by Germany. Many voices—not least that of the IMF— argue, however, that the agreement reached so controversially in July 2015 is absolutely unworkable: Greek debt is astronomical, Greek GDP has fallen so far and fast, Greek banks are so weak and Greek unemployment so high that rational minds see only failure. Many experts are now calling for Greece's creditors to face reality and forego billions of euros of debt—maybe 100 billion. Others see a long-term solution in a political and fiscal union of the Eurozone. Yet this would mean Germany and the other creditors of Greece and Southern European debtor states agreeing to bail them out permanently—hardly the stance they took in the July negotiations. Fiscal federalism in short would come at a huge cost for Germans and there is simply no evidence so far that they are willing to pay it. Maybe it would be easier to expel Greece and others from the Eurozone—a solution that has so far been rejected for political reasons. In any case, whatever the outcome to the present crisis, it seems certain that the Eurozone—if it survives—will be held back economically for decades. Reviewing the sad saga of the Greek crisis in the *London Review of Books* (27 August 2015), the Princeton historian, Jan-Werner Müller, concluded: 'As things stand, the most plausible outcome remains full integration for creditor nations, and a long depression for debtors. Greece could still be forced out; only after the US federal government let some states go bust in the 1840s did its fiscal regime become credible. Things don't have to end with a bang. The EU could slowly fragment, leading to resentment all round.' As for the Eurozone, the highly respected economics editor of the *Sunday Times* David Smith, writing in his weekly column on 19 July 2015, perhaps used understatement when he concluded: 'We should be grateful we are not members of this club.' The American Nobel Prize winner in economics, Paul Krugman, on the other hand, was more blunt in a blog in the New York Times on 17 September 2015: 'The euro area remains a slow-motion disaster, despite the constant claims that a bit of growth here or there somehow vindicates all the suffering.'

The euro, in truth, has failed to achieve all the major objectives which its creators had in mind. It has singularly failed to stop Germany from dominating the EU. It has failed to consolidate the Franco-German partnership. It has failed miserably to replace the dollar as the world's reserve currency—one of the more ambitious motives behind its creation. But most pathetically of all, it has failed even to increase intra-European trade. As David Marsh's points out in his excellent book (Yale University Press, 2013) entitled *Europe's Deadlock. How the Euro Crisis Could Be Solved –and Why It Won't Happen*, the proportion of Germany's total trade within the Eurozone in 2012 (goods exports and imports) was 38%, down from 46% in 1999 when the euro was introduced. The respective figures for other countries were: France down from 52% to 47%, Italy down from 53% to 42%, the Netherlands for 55% to 49% and Spain, down from 59% to 45%. Trade instead was growing with more dynamic economies outside the Eurozone, all of them with different currencies floating against the euro. The point made by Marsh is that the abolition of exchange rates between the countries using the euro brought them no advantage. In his dismissive judgement: 'A common currency is neither a necessary nor a sufficient condition for an effective common market.' Tell that to the federalists!

Apart from the euro, however, the EU faces still other economic problems.

According to data produced by the Research Centre for Generational Contracts ordered by the European Central Bank and published in the *Wall Street Journal* in June 2012, most EU countries owe more than twice their annual GDP in pensions promised to current workers and retirees. The ratios for France, Austria, Germany, Italy, Portugal, Greece, Spain, the Czech Republic, Latvia and the UK respectively are: 362%, 360%, 330%, 323%, 298%, 231%, 204%, 201%, 125%, and 91%. Ageing populations are a further strain. In 2010 the average EU pensioner was supported by almost four workers; by 2050 it will be two.

The current average retirement age is 61 but may have to rise to 75 to make pension costs sustainable. The UK with the lowest pension debt ratio has also been the boldest in reforming its retirement age plans by settling on 68 by 2046, but for the EU as a whole, the National Centre for Policy Analysis estimated in 2009 that the average EU country would need to set aside 8.3% of GDP annually to fund current policies. The implications for growth and investment in the EU are therefore fairly ominous.

Another challenge facing the EU is the cost of green energy. The issue here is not whether one is pro- or anti-Green, sceptical or concerned about global warming but the future economic impact on the EU (and UK) of EU energy policies. Given the EU's dependence on Russia for gas and oil supplies, its energy security remains a major issue.

At present the EU mandates its member states to cut their carbon dioxide emissions 20% by 2020 compared to 1990 levels. The goal after that is to cut emissions by between 80% and 95% by 2050. In May 2010 a study by the European Commission's energy department estimated the 20% cut would cost 48 billion euros annually. The Commission's draft Energy Roadmap for 2050 is frank: 'There is a trade-off between climate change policies and competitiveness.'

This is perhaps an understatement. A report by the UK's Energy Intensive Users Group (representing British businesses) and the TUC cited steel-making, ceramics, paper, cement and lime manufacture, aluminium and basic inorganic chemicals facing up to a 141% in additional energy costs by 2020 as result of carbon dioxide emission schemes. One director of the Group was quoted in the *Wall Street Journal* in 2012 complaining that 'current policies do seem to be angled towards creating a market for overseas competitors.' The UK government admitted that an offshore wind project would cost £140 billion

(£5,600 per household) whereas conventional energy could provide the same amount of energy for 5% of the cost. A report commissioned by the UK's Department of Energy and Climate Change from Professor John Hill of the LSE on fuel poverty—defined as occurring when fuel bills reached 10% of household income—found that by 2016 that the number of households concerned could reach 9.2 million, equivalent to 43% of all homes in the UK. Green taxes and levies are expected to add £200 to bills by 2020. (Britain's Conservative government has now agreed to reverse policy on these taxes.) Again according to the *Wall St. Journal*, Spain's experience of subsidizing renewables has been painful. A 2009 study published by the King Juan Carlos University found that subsidies took up 3.45% of all income tax revenues and been responsible for the loss of 110,500 jobs. An internal review from 2010 by the Zapatero government was also bleak, reporting that the price of Spanish electricity had risen 17% above the European average, owing to the price of subsidized renewables which had quintupled between 2004 and 2010. While Spain has taken some remedial action, Denmark in 2012 had the highest energy prices in Europe. Despite this, the government elected there that year raised its carbon dioxide emission reduction target by 40% by 2020 and set itself the goal of completely phasing out fossil fuels by 2050. Italy's subsidy system meanwhile sets the price floor for wind energy at three times the market level. A study by Italy's Istituto Bruno Leoni found the capital necessary to create one green job could have created 6.9 jobs if invested in industry. Even Germany faces difficulty. Its Energy Feed-in Act of 2000 requiring electric utilities to buy renewables from all producers at fixed, exorbitant rates and feed the electricity into the power grid for 20 years although a Germany utility executive has been quoted saying that solar energy in Germany makes as much sense as growing pineapples in Alaska. Yet Germany now has half the world's solar photovoltaic capacity. Fritz Vahrenholt, a former hero of the German environmental movement now says: 'We're destroying the foundations of our prosperity. In the end what we are doing is putting the German automotive sector at risk, the steel, copper and chemical sectors, silicon, you name it.' France because of its heavy reliance on nuclear power has no emissions problems. But President Hollande has promised to cut nuclear power by a third. His defeated socialist rival to be president, Marine Aubry—author of France's 35 hour week—had promised to eliminate it altogether. It seems that much of Europe wants no part of energy resources even if they are low in carbon dioxide emissions. Thus although Europe has huge shale gas resources, Germany has imposed a moratorium on shale-gas exploration which France already forbids by law. Under Merkel Germany has also abandoned nuclear power. Even in the UK, despite huge reserves of shale gas and the run-down of North Sea oil, it has been extremely difficult to get the process of exploration started. The heading in the article in the *Wall Street Journal* detailing most of this information was 'Europe's Green Energy Suicide'. Remember: the European Commission's own estimate of the cost of its policies is 48 billion euros annually just to reach the 2020 target.

From what has been said already, however, the question arises why anyone in Britain would want to remain part of such an organization. We are not in the Eurozone, so we cannot be subjected to any future plans for political or fiscal union there. So why remain in the EU? For the Common Agricultural Policy which puts up food prices and discriminates against small producers? For the Common Fisheries Policy which has destroyed our fishing fleet and fishing communities, not to mention fish stocks? For a Common Foreign and Security Policy which is an international joke? Or to quote the words of the present President of the European Commission in an interview with *Die Welt am*

Sonntag on 8 March 2015: '...in terms of foreign policy we don't seem to be taken entirely seriously.' *So why do so many British people take the EU so seriously?* After all, when we abandoned empire in the decades after 1945 there was no political or economic trauma or even nostalgia for our long imperial past. Leaving the EU would cause no trauma either and certainly no nostalgia for rule from Brussels. We should have a sense of historical perspective about this. That would also include recognising that at the height of the age of imperialism before 1914 the two countries with the highest standard of living in Europe were Norway and Switzerland, neither of which possessed an empire. And today, again, the two countries with the highest standard of living in Europe are Norway and Switzerland, both outside the EU. Life can be better off without empires or superstate ambitions.

One reason is that many among Britain's financial and economic elites, including advertisers, lawyers and management consultants have grown used to a supranational lifestyle that disconnects them from ordinary mortals. These people make an absolute fortune out of negotiating international contracts and influencing EU directives which multinational corporations with large legal and HR departments can then deploy to squeeze out smaller competing firms and enterprises. These multinationals also use thousands of lobbyists to negotiate special tax breaks ("sweetheart deals") with certain member states –notoriously Belgium, Luxembourg and Ireland—which allow them to pay next to no tax in other member states. Likewise top civil servants and politicians of member states have more in common with one another than with local electorates. Participating in endless meetings in Brussels, where they are put up in five-star hotels, driven around in limos and wined and dined ad nauseam must make their often mundane tasks—agreeing Commission proposals on everything from the size of lawnmower engines to the price of turnips to the size of cod quotas—seem highly significant, although, it is true, that sometimes their decisions can mean life or death for starving Greeks or starving migrants. Little wonder, therefore, that these European elites often seem to dazzle not merely themselves but even outsiders.

Academic research is well aware of the division between the masses and these European elites. In 2012, for example, Oxford University Press published a book entitled *The Europe of Elites. A Study into the Europeanness of Europe's Political and Economic Elites* edited by Heinrich Best and other continental political scientists. It is frankly fairly unreadable but one of its conclusions is to confirm the basic dichotomy between the political elites and the masses: 'The decisive factor distinguishing between the positions of elites and non-elites towards a unified Europe is the empowerment or lack of control that collective actors attribute to a transfer of national responsibilities and authority to the European level.' In other words, the elites want more federalism and the masses less.

Civil servants might be excused for wanting more European control. After all, the EU is run by civil servants, often it seems in their own best interests, and they are remarkably well paid. One fifth of them earn more than the British prime minister. Indeed, according to the London *Times* (4 August 2015), 'Childless EU officials in the "AD II" grade of middle management earn £97,388 and pay tax at 13.4 per cent.' According to the *Daily Telegraph* on 17 August 2015, the average salary of an EU official is thought to be £78,500, taxed at 16%. Just imagine what top ones with families earn. According to the previously quoted article in the *Daily Telegraph*, 13,000 EU employees are issued with special EU credit cards for meals, hotels and incidental expenses while travelling on business. The total bill for these credit cards in 2103 was £85.9 million. 362 officials in Germany alone spent £1.53 million. According to the *Times* (9 November 2016), the cost of servicing EU pensions will go up by 5.2 per cent in 2016. The number of retired EU staff claiming a pension worth 70 per cent of final basic salary is expected to increase by 4 per cent next year, taking the annual bill to 1.6billion euros. The average pension paid to retired European officials is more than 3,000 euros a month and the average retirement age is 61.9 years. (A growing part of the bill is for retired MEPs who under a scheme agreed by the European Parliament in 2009, pay no contributions to their pensions—currently worth 153,760 euros for each five-year term served.) However, instead of dwelling on pay grades, expenses, pensions and holidays (Oh! The holidays!), it is more instructive to examine the attitudes of British civil servants involved with the EU. Here, for example, is an interview with a top foreign office official responsible for key negotiations with Brussels carried out over drinks late at night by Trevor Kavanagh and published on Monday, October 30, 2000 in the *Sun*. Kavanagh was then the political editor of the newspaper. Publication of these interviews is exceptionally rare. But *in vino veritas*.

The interview took place in the context of Tony Blair's desire to have Britain join the euro. The official deeply resented that a promise of a referendum had ever been made: 'There should never have been a promise to hold a referendum. I mean consulting the public on an issue as important as this is barking.' Asked what would happen if a referendum could not be won, he replied: ' Our strategy now is to get us signed up for foreign policy, justice, you name it—so that in the end, joining the euro won't seem like a big deal. It will seem perfectly natural.' He then confessed: 'To me, nationality is an irrelevance,' before adding: 'to be honest, I feel far more comfortable with the mind of people I negotiate with than I do with the "the people".' European mandarins, he claimed, shared 'an outlook, an education, a European culture.

We have far more in common with each other than we do with our respective lower classes.' When Kavanagh suggested he was referring to the kind of people who read the Sun, he replied: 'Exactly. My sister goes out with that sort of scum time after time—very depressing.'

Even more depressing is the thought that the mandarin being interviewed was described by Kavanagh in his article as a '30-something'. He may well, therefore, even today, enjoy a leading role in the negotiations being conducted by David Cameron right now—'very depressing', as he would say.

The British public, of course, is fed a different story about why Britain should continue to support EU membership. Forget for the moment the myths about keeping the peace in Europe since 1945 (What was the threat? How and when did the EU deter it?) and extending democracy (have Hungary, Bulgaria and Romania become model democracies since joining the EU?). These myths will be examined later. No, the real hold, if any that the EU has on the British public mind, is that Britain from the 1870s was a country in relative economic decline and that only membership of the EEC/EU saved it form going under. In fact, the oft-repeated thesis of British decline since 1870 is historical nonsense. As Professor David Edgerton, now Hans Rausing Professor of the History of Science and Technology and Professor of Modern British History at King's College London, and the leading expert in the field, puts it:

'Techno-declinism is, intellectually speaking a nonsense. It produces explanations which, if taken literally, suggest that British science and technology collapsed around 1870. Oddly, most attention has been given to the years before 1914, when Britain was the most industrialized and richest country in Europe and dominated world trade. The international comparisons declinist historians provide are greatly misleading. They usually seek to explain things which were not the case with explanations that don't work.' (Read his *Science, Technology and the British Industrial Decline, 1870-1970.*)

Clearly, Britain at times suffered severe economic challenges. In the 1960s and 1970s these included militant trades unions, high taxes, and high overseas defence expenditure. But all of these were overcome by the actions of British governments. There was no EU input. Again, after the world economic crisis of 2008-9, it was a British government that nationalised some banks and introduced quantitative easing. Again, there was no EU input. Britain's problems were dealt with domestically. Still, according to supporters of the EU, Britain somehow needs the EU to keep her afloat. This may well seem ironic given the catastrophic state of the EU today but its British supporters –the same people who first negotiated dreadful terms of entry in 1972, who then pushed us into membership of the ERM at a cost of many billions of pounds, and who wanted us to join the euro (and still do!)—will never be satisfied till Britain is totally submerged either as a whole or with Scotland and England as separate provinces of a would-be European super-state. Lord Heseltine many years ago told the *Spectator* that he looked forward to the day that the word 'England' would have no more historic resonance or significance than 'Wessex' or 'Mercia' and Richard Branson, the British tax exile, recently explained in the *Times* how much he deplored the prospect of the UK voting to leave the EU and 'going back to being Great Britain'.

The irony of course is that historically Britain has been a great success story, still is in so many ways, and outside the EU could look forward to an even greater future, liberated from the shackles of this declining anachronism. The EU today is in crisis and cannot cope with the many internal and external challenges facing it. It lives off an outdated mythology and has neither democratic credentials nor international influence to boast of. This book has explained the reasons why Britain in the forthcoming referendum should vote to leave it. Nor should there be any fear of isolation when we leave. We would still be in the Security Council of the UNO, the WTO, NATO, the G7 and G20 and a hundred other international organizations. In any case, once we leave, our example will be followed by other states which will envy our new-found independence. The EU has much more to fear from Britain leaving it than do the British themselves.

***

Table of Contents